2.40

BREVILOQUIUM

By

St. Bonaventure

Translated by

Erwin Esser Nemmers, A.M., Mus.M., LL.B.

Formerly Fellow, Harvard University
Lecturer, University of Wisconsin

B. HERDER BOOK CO.
15 & 17 SOUTH BROADWAY, ST. LOUIS 2, MO.
AND
33 QUEEN SQUARE, LONDON, W. C.
1946

NIHIL OBSTAT

G. H. Guyot, C.M.

Censor Librorum

IMPRIMATUR

✠ *Georgius J. Donnelly,*

Administrator,

Sede Vacante

Sti. Ludovici, die 3a Sept. 1946

Vail-Ballou Press, Inc., Binghamton and New York

IN MEMORIAM PATRIS ET MATRIS
HANC TRANSLATIONEM DEDICAT AUCTOR

FOREWORD

St. Bonaventure is better known as a writer than as a person. Considering the influence he exerted on the men of his own generation, both within his order and outside of it, it is strange that we have no contemporary biography of him. Our knowledge of his character and his personality is piecemeal and somewhat fragmentary.

With his works, however, we are more familiar, though even they have not received the attention they deserve, for Bonaventure was a deep and accurate thinker and a prolific writer on a great variety of subjects. It is often said that his duties as General of the Franciscan Order shortened his career as a teacher and restricted the intellectual leadership that he would otherwise have exercised. There is some truth in this contention, for administrative duties, especially of the kind Bonaventure performed for many years and in trying circumstances, are not conducive to productive scholarship. But there is a further and deeper explanation of the fact that Bonaventure has influenced succeeding philosophical thought less consistently and less cogently than has his brilliant friend St. Thomas Aquinas. The latter reared his doctrine on the foundation of Aristotelianism, which was a broader base than the Augustinian tradition on which St. Bonaventure built. Of course Bonaventure was familiar with the teachings of Aristotle, but they did not leave their stamp on his philosophical and mystical thinking as did the doctrines of Augustine. The influence of the latter on the Seraphic Doctor is unquestionable, and Bonaventure was surely a dominant power in the development of the Augustinian thought.

It is in his *Breviloquium* and in his *Commentary on the*

Sentences that St. Bonaventure's dogmatic teachings are expressed most clearly and fully. Hence a translation of the former will be particularly welcomed by those students of medieval philosophy who might find the Latin original too difficult. In presenting this English rendition of the *Breviloquium,* Mr. Nemmers has done a distinct service to the cause of scholarship. It is hoped that the work will receive the cordial and widespread recognition that it merits.

M. Gilson has neatly said that St. Bonaventure is the embodiment of the Franciscan spirit expressing itself "in learning and in constructing its philosophy of the universe under the pressure of its own needs. What St. Francis simply felt and lived, St. Bonaventure was to think" (*The Philosophy of St. Bonaventure,* p. 66).

This first English translation of the *Breviloquium* will help to acquaint its readers with the thought of one of the world's great minds.

Raphael C. McCarthy, S.J.

PREFACE

A word about the principles which have guided this translation is in order. The aim is to render as clearly and accurately as possible the thought of the original. That, despite awkwardness of style which may result, is considered to be the true standard of a translation of philosophy. The difficulties in achieving this aim arise first from the technical nature of the treatise, and secondly from the compactness of thought and expression. Perhaps the difficulty of the present aim is not unrelated to the fact that this work has never before (so far as is known) been translated into any language. And this despite the recognized importance of the work.

My sincere gratitude is due to Dr. John O. Riedl, associate professor of philosophy in Marquette University, who has more than once been both my stimulus and my rescue. In my effort, I have received more than incidental attention from the late Rev. Francis Betten, S.J., the Rev. Charles T. Corcoran, S.J., and particularly from the late Rev. Robert S. Johnston, S.J., all of Marquette University. I am grateful to Father Van de Woestyne, O.F.M., Superior of Collegium S. Bonaventurae, Quarrachi, Italy, for permission to base my translation on the authoritative Quarrachi edition of the *Opera Omnia*.

E. E. N.

INTRODUCTION

St. Bonaventure was born in the year 1221 at Balneumregis, which is today known as Bagnorea, in the vicinity of Viterbo, Italy, and died on July 15, 1274, at Lyons, France. His life span coincides with that of St. Thomas Aquinas, who was born in 1225 (if we accept the more commonly agreed-on date) and died in 1274. St. Bonaventure's father was John Fidanza of Costello, and his mother was Mary Ritella; both were of noble birth. As a baby, Bonaventure (who was named after his father) was presented to St. Francis for his blessing, and the holy founder of the Franciscans, so tradition has it, exclaimed "O buona ventura." However, the name of Bonaventure had been in common use among the Franciscans before John Fidanza was given that name. Occasionally St. Bonaventure is referred to as Jacobus, and as Eustachius or Eutychus, the Greek forms of his name.

St. Bonaventure probably entered the Franciscan Order in 1238 at some novitiate in the Roman province, although there is much dispute as to the date.[1] He was professed in 1239 and then spent the next three years in the study of philosophy. Tradition places the house of studies at Orvieto. In 1242 at the age of twenty-one he was sent to the University of Paris and it is from this time that more certain knowledge of him dates. During the next fifteen years at Paris, he ac-

---

[1] The alternative date given by those who dispute 1238 is 1243. The former date is supported by the Quarrachi editors in *Opera omnia*, X, 40, and by Etienne Gilson, *The Philosophy of St. Bonaventure* (New York: Sheed and Ward, 1938), p. 3. The date 1243 is accepted by P. André Callebaut, O.F.M., "L'éntrée de saint Bonaventure dans l'ordre des Frères Mineurs en 1243," *La France franciscaine* (January–June, 1921), and by P. L. Lemmens, O.F.M., *Der Hl. Bonaventure* (Kempten, 1909). The date is important in determining how long St. Bonaventure was a student under Alexander of Hales and what caused him to follow a different course from St. Thomas Aquinas.

quired the titles by which he is often known in medieval
books. The most common title is *doctor seraphicus;* the less
familiar ones are *doctor devotus* and *doctor mellifluus.* It
was at Paris that St. Bonaventure studied under Alexander
of Hales, *doctor irrefragibilis,* who said of him, "It seems as
though Adam never erred in him." [2] At Paris, St. Bonaventure came in contact with the great philosophers of his day,
notably St. Thomas Aquinas.[3]

At Paris St. Bonaventure spent his first three years (1242–
45) in the study of the Scriptures and the *Quattuor libri sententiarum* of Peter Lombard. In 1245 he took the bachelor's
degree and became lecturer in the house of studies of his
order. After the death of Alexander of Hales in 1245, John
of La Rochelle took the chair of theology. In 1248, St. Bonaventure, after having in that year received his licentiate, suc-
ceeded to this chair. St. Bonaventure taught until 1257, when
he was elected Minister General of the Franciscan Order.
From then on, his life was given largely to administrative
duties which at this time were especially trying because of
the conflict between the regulars and the seculars.[4] It was
because of this conflict that the doctorate was for many years
withheld from St. Bonaventure and St. Thomas. The degree
was finally conferred on both by order of Pope Alexander
IV in 1257.

Almost all St. Bonaventure's philosophical and theological
works were written prior to 1257, and those dealing with the
monastic life, his mystical writings and sermons, largely after
1257. During his generalship he presided at five general chap-

[2] Adam Salimbene, "Catalogus XXIV generalium ministrorum ord. Fr. Min.,"
Analecta Franciscana, III (Quarrachi: Collegium S. Bonaventurae, 1895), 324.

[3] A list of philosophers at the University of Paris at this time is given by
Maurice De Wulf, *Philosophy and Civilization in the Middle Ages* (Princeton:
Princeton University Press, 1922), p. 73.

[4] In defense of the regulars, see St. Bonaventure, *Quaestiones disputatae de
perfectione evangelica;* for the seculars, Guillaume de St. Amour, *De periculis
novissimorum temporum* and, in general, Denifle and Chatelain, *Chartularium
Universitatis Parisiensis* (Paris: Dedelain, 1894–97), I, 247.

ters of the order [5] and supervised the revision of the rules.

In 1265 St. Bonaventure was appointed Archbishop of Paris.[6] For three years after the death of Pope Clement IV in 1268, the cardinals could not agree on a choice for pope. There were six candidates. The cardinals, after summoning St. Bonaventure, bade him name himself or another for the office, and they agreed to ratify his choice. He nominated Theobald of Piacenza, who promptly became Pope Gregory X.[7] St. Bonaventure was made cardinal in 1273. He was canonized in 1482 and made doctor of the Church in 1587.

The works of St. Bonaventure fall naturally into five classes: (1) philosophical and theological treatises, (2) scriptural commentaries, (3) shorter mystical writings, (4) works on the order, and (5) sermons. The list (and dates of writing where known) of those in the first group is:

1. *Commentarii in quattuor libros Petri Lombardi*, 1248–55
2. *Quaestiones disputatae de scientia Christi, de mysterio sanctae Trinitatis, de perfectione evangelica*, before 1257
3. *Breviloquium*, before 1257
4. *Itinerarium mentis in Deum*, October, 1259
5. *De reductione artium ad theologiam*
6. *Collationes in Hexaemeron*, 1273
7. *Collationes de decem donis Spiritus Sancti*, 1268
8. *Collationes de decem praeceptis*, 1267
9. *Sermones selecti de rebus theologicis*

St. Bonaventure's *Breviloquium* (literally "a short treatise") is one of the *Tria opuscula* or "three little works" of a philosophical-theological nature (as distinguished from the *Decem opuscula* which are mystical writings). The other two are the *Itinerarium mentis in Deum* ("The Journey of the

[5] At Narbonne in 1260, at Pisa in 1263, at Paris in 1266, at Assisi in 1269, and at Lyons in 1274.

[6] The bull is in L. Wadding, *Annales minorum* (Quarrachi: Collegium S. Bonaventurae, 1931), IV, 281.

[7] This incident is related by Bartholomew of Pisa, *Conformitates*, conform. 8, p. 2, and is also related in the processes of St. Bonaventure's canonization.

Mind to God") and the *De reductione artium ad theologiam*
("The Reduction of the Arts to Theology").

The authenticity of the *Breviloquium* has never been questioned, according to the Quarrachi editors.[8] There have been
at least 19 editions of the work, and there are extant at least
227 codices containing it. It has been more often printed
than any other work of St. Bonaventure, with the possible
exception of his *Life of St. Francis.*[9] The best estimate of the
date of its writing is shortly before 1257,[10] and since he completed his *Commentarii in quattuor libros Petri Lombardi*
in 1255, quite possibly the *Breviloquium* was written between
1255 and 1257, for the internal structure of the work seems
to indicate that it is a compendium of the *Commentarii*. The
Breviloquium is much shorter than the *Commentarii*, and
the arguments are mere sketches compared with those in the
larger work. St. Bonaventure himself describes his purpose:
"Upon the request of my associates that from my poor knowledge I say something briefly in a *summa* about the truths of
theology, and conquered by their prayers, I have consented
to set down a kind of compendium in which I do not deal
with all matters summarily, but treat briefly certain matters
that it is more important to know, including at the same time
such explanation for their understanding as may come to
mind at the moment." [11]

The viewpoint from which the work is developed is de-
ducing all from the first principle.[12] This is in contrast to
the *De reductione artium ad theologiam* which reduces all to

---

[8] Bonaventure, *Opera omnia*, V, prolegomena, c. 3. Cf. Bernard Geyer,
Friedrich Ueberwegs Grundriss der Geschichte der Philosophie (Berlin: E. S.
Mittler & Sohn, 1928), Zweiter Teil, "Die patristische und scholastische Philoso-
phie," pp. 386–96, 733–38.

[9] Cf. Bonaventure, *Opera omnia*, V, xvi–xxvi, and X, 10.

[10] Cf. *Opera omnia*, X, 10, where it is stated that the text in one of the oldest
codices bears the date 1257.

[11] Bonaventure, *Breviloquium*, prologue, § 6, 5.

[12] *Ibid.*, § 6, 6.

the first principle as does the *Itinerarium mentis in Deum.* There is no need to synopsize the *Breviloquium* since the index of parts and chapters suffices for that. The chief philosophical doctrines which it treats of are: faith and reason, creation, the *rationes seminales,* the doctrine of *lumen,* moral and intellectual illumination, the so-called ontologism of St. Bonaventure's proofs of God's existence, the attributes of God, grace and free will, the Victorine doctrine of the eye of the flesh, the eye of reason, and the eye of contemplation, the Neoplatonic conception of the universe, and many other doctrines.

These doctrines become more intelligible when one views them in the light of their sources. Chief among these is St. Augustine. But also strongly represented are: St. Ambrose, St. Anselm, Aristotle, Avicenna, St. Bernard of Clairvaux, Boethius, Cicero, St. Gregory, Hilary, St. John Damascene, Pseudo-Dionysius, St. Gregory, St. Jerome, Plato, and Hugh and Richard of St. Victor. Nor is St. Bonaventure chary in acknowledging his debt to them. He tells which authors he finds most able and in what fields they excel:

Regarding the first (faith) one ought to work hard in the study of the doctors, regarding the second (morals) in the study of the preachers, regarding the third (the end of both faith and morals) in the study of the contemplatives. The first subject Augustine teaches best, the second Gregory, the third Dionysius (Pseudo). Anselm follows Augustine, Bernard follows Gregory, and Richard (of St. Victor) follows Dionysius. Anselm is interested in reasoning, Bernard in preaching, and Richard in contemplation—Hugh (of St. Victor) is interested in them all.[13]

But Augustine is the court of last resort: "This view I believe ought to be held not only because reason convinces us but because the authority of St. Augustine confirms it." [14]

[13] Bonaventure, *De reductione artium ad theologiam,* § 5, in finem.
[14] Bonaventure, *Commentarii in quattuor libros sententiarum,* II, 7, 2, 2, q. 2 conclu.

Contrary to the opinion of some writers,[15] St. Bonaventure knew Greek philosophy. He repeatedly quotes Aristotle and recognizes him as the great non-Christian mind.[16] He did, however, reject the whole Aristotelian approach of St. Thomas. As Gilson says, "From his first contact with the pagan thought of Aristotle, St. Bonaventure is as one who has understood, seen through it, and passed beyond it." [17]

The question whether theology and philosophy should be separate had been raised by St. Albert the Great and answered in the affirmative by him and by St. Thomas. Answering in the negative were Alexander of Hales and St. Bonaventure.

With the growth of Averroism on the one hand, and Thomism on another, the position of St. Bonaventure was strongly attacked. This led him to take up again toward the end of his life the subjects of philosophy and theology. He began the *Collationes in Hexaemeron* in the winter of 1273 (only to have death cut this work short) to make his position doubly clear and convincing. St. Bonaventure placed Christ in the center of philosophy as well as of theology. He argued that philosophy without the assistance of theology was incompetent to achieve truth, at least it was incompetent in the field of natural religion, or as it is otherwise known, natural theology. And here St. Bonaventure calls history to witness. Had any man before Christ ever achieved truth? Even the best, and this was Aristotle, could not so much as be sure that he had arrived at one God, much less undertake the problem of His attributes. Unless man keeps his eyes set beyond the

---

[15] Including even the scholiasts of Quarrachi. Cf. Gilson, *La philosophie de Saint Bonaventure* (Paris: Librarie J. Vrin, 1924), p. 11, note 3. This note is omitted in the English edition.

[16] E.g., *Commentarii in quattuor libros sententiarum*, II, 1, 1, 1, q. 1 "(Aristotelis) fuit princeps et dux peripateticorum." *Ibid.*, q. 2 concl.: "(Aristotelis) fuit excellentior inter philosophos." But Aristotle is not to be compared with Christian thinkers. *Sermo* IV, par. 18: "(Aristotelis) stabiliebat viam scientiae, superiore sapientiae neglecta," and *ibid.* later: "principaliter aspiciebat ad inferiorem."

[17] Gilson, *The Philosophy of St. Bonaventure*, p. 5.

CONTENTS

PROLOGUE

PART I

THE TRINITY OF GOD

PART II

THE CREATION OF THE WORLD

PART III

THE CORRUPTION OF SIN

PART IV

THE INCARNATION OF THE WORD

CONTENTS xxi

CONTENTS

PART VII

THE FINAL JUDGMENT

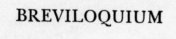

BREVILOQUIUM

PROLOGUE

1. "For this cause I bow my knees to the Father of our Lord Jesus Christ, of whom all paternity in heaven and earth is named: that He would grant you, according to the riches of His glory, to be strengthened by His Spirit with might unto the inward man: that Christ may dwell by faith in your hearts; that, being rooted and founded in charity, you may be able to comprehend, with all the saints, what is the breadth and length and height and depth; to know also the charity of Christ, which surpasseth all knowledge, that you may be filled unto all the fullness of God." [1]

The great doctor of the nations and preacher of truth, filled with the divine Spirit, the vessel chosen and sanctified, discloses in these words the source, growth, and result of Holy Scripture, which is called theology. He notes that the source of Scripture is discovered in the influence of the Most Blessed Trinity, its growth is in the exigency of one's human capability, and its result or fruit, is in an abundance of the fullest happiness.

2. The source of Scripture is not attributable to human investigation, but to divine revelation which flows "from the Father of lights" [2] from whom all paternity in heaven and earth is named, and from whom through His Son, Jesus Christ, the Holy Ghost flows into us, and through the Holy Ghost, dividing and distributing His gifts to individuals as He pleases, faith is given to us, and through faith Christ dwells in our hearts. This is the knowledge of Jesus Christ from whom the strength and understanding of the whole of

[1] Eph. 3:14–19.
[2] Jas. 1:17.

3

Holy Scripture flows as from its source. Hence it is impossible that anyone should enter into that knowledge unless he first have infused into himself faith in Christ, the light, the door, and the very foundation of all Scripture. This is the faith of all supernatural illuminations as long as we are absent from the Lord [3] and the foundation that stabilizes us, the light that directs us, and the door that lets us in. Further, according to the measure of faith the wisdom given us by God must be determined lest anyone "be more wise than it behooveth to be wise, but to be wise unto sobriety and according as God hath divided to every one the measure of faith." [4] Through the medium of that faith, a knowledge of Sacred Scripture is given to us in accordance with the influence of the Blessed Trinity, as the Apostle expressly states in the first part of the reference cited above. [5]

3. The growth of Holy Scripture is not restricted to the laws of reasoning, defining, and dividing, after the custom of the other sciences, nor is it limited to a part of the universe. Rather, since it proceeds in accord with supernatural light to give to man as wayfarer a sufficient knowledge of things that expedite salvation, it describes partly in common words and partly in mystical words and, as it were, in a kind of summa the contents of the whole universe, in which the breadth is considered; it describes the course, in which the length is considered; it describes the excellence of those who are finally to be saved, and in this the sublimity is considered; it describes the misery of those who are to be damned, and in this consists the depth not only of the universe itself but also of the divine judgment. Thus it describes the whole universe so far as it is expedient to have a knowledge of it for salvation: according to its length and breadth, height and depth. Scripture in its growth has the four qualities that will

---

[3] II Cor. 5:6.
[4] Rom. 12:3.
[5] Cf. *supra*, the first paragraph of this Prologue.

be declared below. Human capacity plays a part in that it is born to grasp magnificently and in many ways great and numerous ideas. As it were, there is born in man a certain most noble mirror in which the universality of earthly things is reflected naturally and even supernaturally so that the growth of Sacred Scripture is considered according to the exigency of human capacity.

4. The result or fruit of Holy Scripture is not simply any kind, but rather a fullness of eternal happiness. In Scripture are the words of eternal life. It is written not only that we may believe, but also that we may possess eternal life, in which we shall see and love, and our desires will be completely satisfied. When these desires are satisfied, we shall know the overwhelming love of knowledge and thus we shall abound unto all the fullness of God. Divine Scripture tries to lead us on to this plenitude in accord with the truth of the sentence of the Apostle quoted above.[6] This, then, is the end and this the intention with which Holy Scripture should be studied, taught, and even heard.

5. That we may arrive at that fruit by progress along the true path of the Scriptures, we must make a solemn invocation: that we may ascend with true faith to the Father of lights by bending the knee of our heart and that through His Son in the Holy Ghost, He may grant us true knowledge of Jesus Christ and with this knowledge a love of Him, and that, knowing and loving Him and finally achieving a solid faith and a deep-rooted love, we may be able to know the length and breadth, height and depth, of Holy Scripture, and through this knowledge arrive at the fullness of knowledge and plenitude of love for the Most Blessed Trinity whence the desires of all holy men tend and in whom is found the end and complement of all truth and goodness.

6. Since the end of Sacred Scripture is desired and known, and since its beginning is believed and the invocation made,

[6] *Ibid.*

we may view its course according to its length and breadth, height and depth, following the path and the order of the apostolic document. The breadth of Scripture consists of the multiplicity of its parts, the length in the description of the times and ages, the height in the description of the hierarchies arranged in different levels, and the depth in the multiplicity of the mystical senses and intelligences.

Section One

The Breadth of Holy Scripture

1. If we wish to behold the breadth of Holy Scripture, the first viewpoint available to us is Scripture divided into two Testaments, namely, the Old and the New. The Old is replete with many books, for it has the books of laws, of history, of wisdom, and of the prophets. Of the first there are five, of the second ten, of the third five, and of the fourth six, and hence in all there is a total of twenty-six books. Similarly, the New Testament has books corresponding to these and also arranged in a fourfold division. The evangelical books correspond to the books of the laws, the Acts of the Apostles to the historical books, the letters of the Apostles, especially those of Paul, to the books of wisdom, and the Apocalypse to the prophetical books. Thus the remarkable conformity between the Old and the New Testament may be seen not only in consistency of meanings, but also in their fourfold division. In this grouping and arrangement, Ezechiel [7] sees four wheels of faces and a wheel in the midst of the wheel, because the Old is in the New, and the New is in the Old. In the books of the laws and in the evangelical books is the face of a lion because of his powerful authority. In the historical books is the face of a bull because of his convincing strength. In the books of wisdom is the face of a man because

---

[7] Ezech. 1:15.

of his nice prudence. In the books of the prophets is the face of the eagle because of his perspicacious insight.

2. Holy Scripture is correctly divided into the Old and the New Testament and not into practical and speculative, as in the case of philosophy. The reason for this is that, since Scripture deals properly with what is known by faith which is the strength and foundation of morals, justice and all right living, it follows that there cannot be found in Scripture a knowledge of things as such, or of moral rules based on such a knowledge. This is not, however, the case with philosophy, which treats of the truth of morals and gives consideration to pure speculation. Because Holy Scripture is a knowledge moving toward good and withdrawing from evil, and this is accomplished both by fear and by love, it follows that Scripture is divided into two Testaments, for there is "a narrow margin between fear and love." [8]

3. Because man can be moved in a fourfold manner toward good and away from evil, namely, by precepts of a most powerful authority, by the statements of a most wise truth, by the examples and benefits of a most innocent goodness, or by all of these taken together, it follows that the books handed down to us containing the Holy Scripture should be divided into four groups in the New as well as in the Old Testament to achieve a correspondence with the four methods just outlined. Accordingly, the books of laws move men by the precepts of a most potent authority, the historical books by the examples of a most innocent goodness, the books of wisdom by the statements of a most prudent truth, the prophetical books by a combination of all of these, as clearly appears in their respective contents. Hence these books are, as it were, commemorative of all true wisdom and doctrine.

4. Sacred Scripture is like a very wide river which grows continually in size by the addition of many tributaries as its course lengthens. In the beginning of Scripture are the books

[8] Augustine, *Contra Adimantum*, XVII, 2.

of the laws, then is added the stream of wisdom found in the
historical books, and thirdly the doctrine of Solomon the most
wise, and after these the doctrine of the holy prophets; and
finally the evangelical doctrine is revealed, spread through the
mouth of the living Christ, written by the Evangelists, and
propagated by the holy apostles together with additional docu-
ments which the Holy Ghost, coming down upon them, taught
us through them. Thus the apostles, having been taught all
truth by the Holy Ghost according to the divine promise,
could give the Church of Christ the doctrine of all-saving
truth and, by completing Holy Scripture, might enlarge the
knowledge of truth.

Section Two

The Length of Holy Scripture

1. Holy Scripture has a length which consists of the description of the times and ages, namely, from the beginning of the
world to the day of judgment. It describes the course of the
world through three times: the time of the law of nature, the
time of the written law, and the time of the law of grace. But
in the three times, it distinguishes seven ages. Of these, the
first is from Adam to Noe, the second from Noe to Abraham,
the third from Abraham to David, the fourth from David to
the transmigration of Babylon, the fifth from the transmigration to Christ, the sixth from Christ to the end of the world;
the seventh, which runs concurrently with the sixth, begins
with the repose of Christ in the sepulcher and runs to the universal resurrection which marks the beginning of the eighth.
Thus Scripture is of great length because in its treatment it
begins with the commencement of the world and of time, in
the beginning of Genesis, and extends to the end of the world
and of time, namely, to the end of the Apocalypse.

2. To be correct, universal time, which runs according to
a triple law, that is, founded within, given externally, and in-

fused from above, extends through seven ages and ends with the end of the sixth age. Hence the duration of the world follows a plan such that the duration of the greater world corresponds with the duration of the life of the lesser world, namely, man, for whom the greater world was made.

The first age of the world, in which the foundation of the world, the fall of the demons, and the strengthening of the angels were completed, corresponds to the first day when light was made distinct from darkness. The second age, in which through the ark and flood the good were saved and the evil destroyed, corresponds to the second day when throughout the firmament a distinction was made of the waters from the waters. The third age, in which Abraham was called and the synagogue begun, which was to bring forth fruit and generate a posterity for the worship of God, corresponds to the third day, when land appeared and brought forth green vegetation. The fourth age, in which the kingdom and the priesthood grew powerful because King David expanded divine worship, corresponds to the fourth day, in which the formation of the suns and stars took place. The fifth age, in which the emigrants were scattered and spread through many nations, corresponds to the fifth day, in which the production of the fishes from the waters was accomplished. The sixth age, in which Christ who is truly the image of God was born in the form of man corresponds to the sixth day, in which the first man was made. The seventh age, which is the endless rest of souls, corresponds to the seventh day, on which God rested from all His work which He had done.

3. Thus seven ages are distinguished by the signs which are found in their beginning and by reason of which they correspond to the days of the foundation of the world. The first is called the age of infancy because, as our whole infancy is drowned in oblivion, so that first age was drowned by the flood. The second age is childhood because, as in childhood we begin to speak, so in the second age the multiplication of

tongues was accomplished. The third age is called adolescence because, as the generative force begins to be actualized at that time, so Abraham was called and circumcision given him and the promise made to him about his seed. The fourth age is called manhood because, as in the period of manhood the age of man flowers, so in the fourth age the synagogue flourished under the kings. The fifth age is called old age because, as man's powers decline in old age and beauty slips away, so in the migration there was a decline in the sacred rites of the Jews. The sixth age is called debility because, as that age is linked with death though possessing the mighty light of wisdom, so the sixth age of the world ends with the day of judgment and in it wisdom grows strong through the doctrine of Christ.

4. Thus the whole world is described in a most orderly sequence by Scripture as proceeding from beginning to end, in accordance with the peculiar beauty of its well-designed song. One can view, following the sequence of time, the variety, multiplicity and symmetry, order, rectitude and beauty of the many judgments proceeding from the wisdom of God governing the world.[9] As no one can see the beauty of a song unless his view extends over the whole verse, so no one sees the beauty of the order and governance of the universe unless he beholds the whole of it. Because no man is so long-lived that he can see the whole of it with the eyes of the flesh and because no man can foresee the future by himself, the Holy Ghost has provided man with Holy Scripture, the length of which is measured by the extent of the universe.

Section Three

The Height of Holy Scripture

1. Holy Scripture in its progress possesses a height which consists of the description of the hierarchies arranged in

9 Cf. Augustine, *Epistle* 138 (alias 5), I, 5.

grades. These hierarchies are: the ecclesiastical, the angelical, and the divine, or in other words, the subcelestial, the celestial, and the supercelestial. Scripture describes the first clearly, the second somewhat more obscurely, and the third more obscurely still. From the description of the ecclesiastical hierarchy, we gather that it is lofty, and from the description of the angelic that it is loftier still, and from the description of the divine that it is the highest loftiness, so that we can quote that saying of the Prophet: "Thy knowledge is become wonderful to me; it is high, and I cannot reach to it." [10]

2. This view has supporting evidence. Since things have existence in matter, they should have existence in spirit through acquired knowledge, have existence in that spirit through grace, have existence in it through glory, and have existence in the eternal art. Philosophy treats of things as they are in nature, or in spirit, according to naturally founded knowledge or even acquired knowledge; but theology, in the last analysis knowledge founded on faith and revealed through the Holy Ghost, deals with those matters which concern grace and glory, and even eternal Wisdom. Whence it is that theology relegates philosophical knowledge to a lower place and assumes about the nature of things whatever is needed for fabricating the mirror through which a representation of things divine takes place. It erects a ladder, as it were, which touches the earth at its base but touches heaven at its top. All this is done through that one hierarch, Jesus Christ, who by reason of the human nature He assumed is a hierarch not only in the ecclesiastical hierarchy, but also in the angelic hierarchy, and the middle person in that supercelestial hierarchy of the Most Blessed Trinity. Thus through Him from the very height of God, sanctifying grace descends not only to the beard but also to the skirt of the garment,[11] not only to lofty Jerusalem but to the Church militant.

10 Ps. 138:6.
11 Ps. 132:2.

3. There is a great beauty in the mechanism of the world, but there is far greater beauty in the Church adorned with the beauty of the holy charismata, and the greatest beauty in lofty Jerusalem, and yet the very greatest beauty is to be found in the Trinity, most high and blessed. Hence the Scripture not only possesses the highest matter through which it causes delight and raises aloft the understanding of the mind, but it also is the most elegant matter and in a certain remarkable manner pleases our intellect and thus more and more by such pleasure makes us accustomed to the intuitions and analogies of the divine spectacles.

Section Four

The Depth of Holy Scripture

1. Lastly, Holy Scripture possesses a depth which consists in the multiplicity of the mystical intelligences. Besides a literal sense, it possesses diverse places capable of triple construction, namely, allegorical, moral, and anagogical. It is allegory when through one fact another fact is indicated, according to what must be believed. We have a tropological or moral sense when, through what took place, we are given to understand something else, which must be done. We have an anagogical sense, a kind of leading upwards, when we are given to understand what should be sought after, namely, the eternal happiness of the saints.

2. Hence this threefold meaning ought to exist in Scripture in addition to the literal meaning, because it satisfies the subject of Scripture, its reader or disciple, its origin, and finally its end. I say that it satisfies the subject because its doctrine deals with God and Christ, with the works of reparation and with what should be believed. The subject of Scripture, so far as it is a substance, is God, so far as it is virtue, is Christ, and so far as it is an operation, is the work of reparation. So far as it is all these things, Scripture is subject to belief. More-

over, God is three and one: one in essence and three in person. Hence Scripture, which is about God, has in the unity of its words a threefold meaning. The same is true of Christ. Since there is one Word, all things are said to have been accomplished through Him and reflect unto Him so that His wisdom is multiform and one. The works of reparation, though they are many, all have an aspect pointing to the oblation of Christ. What should be believed, as a thing believable, is reflected in many ways in accord with the different station of the believers. Because of its conformity to all that has been pointed out, Holy Scripture produces multiform meaning in one set of words.

3. This qualifies a hearer: namely, that no one is a suitable hearer unless he is humble, clean, faithful, and zealous. Hence under the bark of the evident meaning is hidden a mystical and profound meaning to repress one's pride so that by the profundity lying in the humility of the word, the proud are rebuffed, the unclean are repulsed, the deceitful are turned aside, and the careless are spurred on to the meaning of the mysteries. Because those hearing the doctrine of Scripture are not of one kind but may be of any kind, for it behooves all who want to be saved to know something of this doctrine, it follows that Scripture has a multiform meaning. Thus it may capture every intellect and may equally illumine and inflame every intellect striving diligently to understand it by the multiformity of its resplendence.

4. Scripture satisfies the principle from which it comes because it is from God through Christ and the Holy Ghost speaking by the mouths of the prophets and the others who wrote the document. Because God speaks not only through words but also through deeds, as in Him to say is to do, and to do is to say, and further, because all things created, as effects of God, point to their cause, it follows that in Scripture the truths divinely handed down ought to be signified not only by words but also by deeds. Because Christ is a doctor

though He was humble in flesh but mighty in His deity, it is suitable for Him and His doctrine to have a humility in speech with a profundity of meaning, so that, as Christ was wrapped in swaddling clothes, so the wisdom of God in the Scriptures is wrapped in certain humble figures. The Holy Ghost in many ways illuminated and made revelations in the hearts of the prophets. No intellect can lie hidden from Him, and He was sent to teach all truth. Thus it belongs to His teaching that in one speech many meanings are hidden.

5. Yet Scripture is suited to its purpose because it was given so that through it man may be guided in knowing and doing things to enable him finally to obtain what should be desired. Because all creatures were made to serve man in his effort toward his home above, Scripture considers various species of creatures so that through them it may teach us the wisdom guiding us to things eternal. And because man is not guided to things eternal unless he knows the things to be known as the truth to be believed and performs the good to be performed as the good that ought to be done and directs his desires to seeing, to loving, and to enjoying God, Holy Scripture, given through the Holy Ghost, considers the book of creation by referring to the end with a triple meaning so that through the tropological sense we may have a list of things to be done energetically, through the allegorical sense we may have an indication of the things to be believed truly, and through the anagogical sense a list of things to be sought out for our enjoyment. And all this so that, sanctified through powerful influences, illuminated through resplendent faith, and perfected through a most ardent charity, we may at last obtain the reward of eternal happiness.

Section Five

The Mode of Proceeding in Holy Scripture

1. Hence in such a multiformity of wisdom as is contained in the length, breadth, height, and depth of Holy Scripture,

there is one common mode of proceeding, the authentic as it were, and within this is the narrative mode, the instructive, the prohibitive, the hortatory, the commendatory, the threatening, the promising, the deprecative, and the laudatory. All these modes are resolved into one authentic mode and rightly so.

2. Since this doctrine exists that we may become good and be saved and this in turn may not be accomplished merely through intellectual considerations but rather through inclinations of the will, divine Scripture ought to be propounded in such a way that we can be the more strengthened in our inclinations. Because our desire is better stimulated through examples than through arguments, better through promises than through reasonings, better through devotions than through definitions, Scripture ought not to have a mode based on definition, division, and integration, for the stimulation of certain powers of the reader in the manner of the other sciences, but ought to have modes proper to itself, following the various inclinations which propel the soul in diverse ways. And all this, so that if anyone is not moved through precepts and prohibitions, he may at least be moved by the examples narrated; if anyone is not moved by the examples, he may be moved by the benefits which are made plain to him; if anyone is unmoved by either of these, he may be moved by the wise admonitions, by the truthful promises, and by the terrible threats, so that thus at least he may be aroused to the worship and praise of God in whom he perceives the grace to guide him to virtuous acts.

3. Because these modes of narration cannot follow the path of the certainty of reason since particular acts cannot be tested, it follows that, lest Scripture should vacillate in doubt and consequently convince us less forcefully, God provided Scripture with the certainty of authority in place of the certainty of reason, and this certainty of authority is great enough that it surpasses all the acuteness of human ability. The authority of one who can deceive or be deceived is not a certain

authority; and, except God and the Holy Ghost, no one is
ignorant that he can deceive and be deceived. Therefore it follows that, inasmuch as Holy Scripture should be perfectly authentic in its own proper way, it has been handed down not
through human investigation but through divine revelation.

4. Hence nothing should be despised in Holy Scripture as
useless, nothing rejected as false, nothing repudiated as wicked,
because the Holy Ghost, its most perfect author, could speak
nothing false, nothing superfluous, nothing too insignificant.
"Heaven and earth shall pass: but My words (of Holy Scripture) shall not pass" [12] until they are fulfilled. "Till heaven
and earth pass, one jot or one tittle shall not pass of the law,
till all be fulfilled," as the Savior has testified. "He therefore
that shall break" the teaching of Scripture . . . "and shall so
teach men, shall be called the least in the kingdom of heaven.
But he that shall do and teach, he shall be called great in the
kingdom of heaven." [13]

Section Six

The Manner of Explaining Holy Scripture

1. As Scripture has a special mode of proceeding, it ought
to be understood and explained in a special way according to
its mode of proceeding. Since under one word Scripture can
shield a multiplicity of meaning, the one who explains Scripture ought to bring the hidden meaning to light and to make
manifest what is brought to light through other more evident scriptural passages. Thus, if I should explain that passage of the Psalms: "Take hold of arms and shield; and rise up
to help me," [14] and if I wish to explain what the divine arms
are, I should say that they are its truth and good will. That

12 Matt. 24:35.
13 Matt. 5:18 f.
14 Ps. 34:2.

this is so must be proven through other scriptural evidence, for it is written in another place: "Thou hast crowned us, as with a shield of Thy good will"; [15] and again: "His truth shall encompass thee with a shield." [16] No one can develop such a facility except by long practice in reading the text of the Bible and committing it to memory; otherwise he will never be able to be expert in the exposition of the Scriptures. Hence, just as he who declines to acquire the first elements out of which speech is constructed, will never be able to understand the meaning of spoken things or the right rules of construction, so he who spurns the letter of Holy Scripture will never rise to its spiritual meanings.

2. The one who explains Scripture should recognize that not all the explanations are allegorical and that not all things need to be explained as mystical. For this purpose, we should note that Holy Scripture has four parts. In the first there is a literal treatment of earthly natures. In this manner Scripture handles our reparation as is apparent in the description of the formation of the world. In the second there is a treatment of the doings and wanderings of the people of Israel and in this way Scripture indicates the reparation of mankind. In the third part there is a treatment in plain words which express what is pertinent to our salvation with regard to faith or morals. The fourth part is that in which Scripture treats of the mystery of our salvation, partly in plain words and partly in enigmatic and obscure words. Hence Scripture does not have a uniform exposition in these various places.

3. It behooves the one who is explaining to be guided in the exposition of Holy Scripture by the triple rule which can be drawn from the words of Augustine in the book *De doctrina christiana*.[17]

The first rule is this: Wherever in Scripture the immediate

---

[15] Ps. 5:13.
[16] Ps. 90:5.
[17] Augustine, *De doctrina christiana*, III, 10, 14.

meaning of the words points to matters of creation, or individual acts of human intercourse, the very things designated by the words are first implied and then the mysteries of our reparation, and where the primary meaning of the words indicates faith or charity, no allegory should be sought.

The second rule is this: Where the words of Scripture designate matters of creation or of the practices of the people of Israel, one should inquire from another source in Scripture what the meaning may be, and finally he may elicit the meaning through words patently indicating a truth of faith or a rule of morals so that if it be said that sheep beget twins,[18] it is clear that sheep there signifies man, and twins signifies a dual charity.

The third rule is this: Wherever a part of Scripture has a kind of literal and spiritual meaning, the one who is explaining ought to determine whether the attributed meaning serves a historical or a spiritual purpose, unless perchance it is incapable of serving either. If, however, it fits both, then there ought to be affirmation of its literal and spiritual meaning, but if only a single purpose is indicated, there should be only a spiritual interpretation: just as the statements that the sabbath of the law is perpetual, the priesthood is eternal, the possession of the land is eternal, and the rule of circumcision is eternal, all have reference to a spiritual meaning.

4. In order that a person may invade the forest of Holy Scripture with security in investigation and exposition, it is first necessary that he know the truth of Holy Scripture in explicit words, that is, that he ascertain how Scripture describes the beginning, progress, and consummation of the two groups: of those looking on themselves contrariwise, namely, of the good who humble themselves here that they may be eternally exalted in the future, and of the wicked who exalt themselves here that they may be eternally humbled. Hence Scripture treats of the whole universe as regards height and

18 Cant. 4:2.

depth, first and last, and as regards an intermediate course under the form of a certain intelligible cross in terms of which the whole mechanism of the universe has to be described and in a certain way seen by the light of the mind. To understand this we must know the principle of things, God, the creation of those things, their fall, their redemption through the blood of Jesus Christ, their rehabilitation through grace, their cure through the sacraments, and finally their retribution through punishment and eternal glory.

5. Because this doctrine has been handed down so diffusely in the writings of the saints and even of the doctors that it cannot be understood or comprehended for a long time by those willing to listen to Holy Scripture—and for this reason even the new theologians frequently distort Holy Scripture into an uncertain, disordered and almost obscure forest—and upon the request of my associates that from my poor knowledge I say something briefly in a *summa* about the truths of theology, and won by their prayers, I have consented to set down a kind of compendium in which I do not deal with all things summarily, but treat briefly of certain things that it is more important to know, including at the same time such explanation for their understanding as may come to mind at the moment.

6. Because theology is discourse about God and about the first principle, and because that science and most noble doctrine resolves all in God as in the first and supreme principle, it follows that in the assignment of reasons in all matters contained in this entire little tract, I have tried to undertake my reasoning from the first principle, that thus I might show that the truth of Holy Scripture is by God, from God, in accord with God, and because of God, so that this science may deservedly appear to be a single and orderly science and not undeservedly be named theology. If, therefore, anything imperfect, obscure, superfluous, or not quite correct is there, it may be due to faulty workmanship, the brevity of time, and

the poverty of knowledge; if there is anything correct, honor and glory should be referred to God alone.

In order that what follows may be made more clear, I have taken the trouble to set down the particular chapter headings to aid the memory and clarify the understanding of what is said. The work is divided into seven parts and seventy-two chapters.[19]

[19] This list of headings is here omitted. It is contained in the table of contents *supra*.

The end of the prologue.

PART ONE

THE TRINITY OF GOD

CHAPTER ONE

A SUMMARY OF THE SEVEN TOPICS WITH WHICH THEOLOGY DEALS

1. At the outset, we must understand that sacred doctrine, namely, theology, deals principally with the first principle, namely, God triune and one, and discusses in the main seven topics: first, the Trinity of God; second, the creation of the world; third, the corruption of sin; fourth, the incarnation of the Word; fifth, the grace of the Holy Ghost; sixth, the sacramental remedy; and seventh, the state of the final judgment.

2. The explanation of this truth is as follows: Because Sacred Scripture or theology is a study giving an idea of the first beginning adequate enough for the state of the wayfarer, and this is according to what is necessary for salvation, and because God is not only the beginning of things and the exemplar operative in the act of creation, but also restorative in the redemption and perfective in retribution, theology treats of God the Creator, of the act of creation and of the creature. And also, because the rational creature who is in a certain sense the end of all, did not persist in good, but because of its fall needed to be restored, it follows that theology deals with the corruption of sin, the physician, the state of health, and the remedy, and finally with the completed healing which will be in glory after the wicked have been hurled to their punishment. Finally, it follows that theology alone is a perfect science because it begins from the beginning, which is the first principle, and continues to the very end, namely, the everlasting reward. It begins with the highest, which is Almighty God, Creator of all, and extends to the very lowest, which is infernal punishment.

3. Theology alone is perfect wisdom because it starts from the highest cause as the beginning of things caused, beyond where philosophical knowledge ceases, and proceeds through this cause in its role as the remedy of sinners and leads back to it as the reward of the deserving ones and the culmination of desires. In this knowledge there is perfect taste, life, and salvation of souls, and consequently the desire of all Christians should be inflamed to its attainment.

4. From all these statements, it is evident that, although theology treats of many and varied topics, it is a united science whose subject is God as He from whom all things have existence, Christ as He through whom all things are, the work of reparation as that toward which all things are directed, the singular bond of charity by which heavenly and earthly things are joined as that about which all things are united, the credible in so far as it is credible as that about which all things are contained in the canonical books, the credible in so far as it is intelligible as that about which all things are contained in the expository books. All this is in accord with Augustine, who says in the *De utilitate credendi:* [1] "What we believe, we owe to authority; what we understand, we owe to reason."

CHAPTER TWO

THE CORRECT VIEW OF THE TRINITY OF THE PERSONS AND THE UNITY OF THE ESSENCE

1. We must therefore give consideration to three aspects of the Trinity of God, namely, how the unity of substance and nature is at the same time compatible first with the plurality

---

[1] Augustine, *De utilitate credendi*, II, 25.

of persons, second with the plurality of apparitions, and third with the plurality of appropriations.

2. Faith directs that we hold this about the plurality of persons: in the unity of nature there are three persons, the Father, the Son, and the Holy Ghost. Of these the first proceeds from nothing, the second from the first alone through generation, and the third from the first and second by spiration or procession.[2] Thus the Trinity of the persons does not exclude from the divine essence perfect unity, simplicity, immensity, eternity, immutability, necessity, and even primacy, but rather the more includes perfect fecundity, love, liberality, equality, interrelationship, likeness, and inseparability. All these things true faith understands to be present in the Most Blessed Trinity.

3. The explanation of this truth is: Faith, since it is the beginning of the cultivation of God and the foundation of "that doctrine which is according to godliness,"[3] directs that a person's thought about God should be in the highest and best manner. However, a person's thought would not be in the best manner if he did not believe that God is able to communicate Himself in the best way. A person would not be thinking in the most virtuous manner if he believed that God was able but unwilling to do so. Hence that one may think in the best and most virtuous manner, faith says that God communicates Himself in the best manner by eternally having a loved one and another beloved of these two, and hence God is one and triune.

4. To this tenet of faith, in so far as it directs one to think of God in a most virtuous manner, the whole of Sacred Scripture, which is said to be the doctrine in accord with godliness,[4] bears testimony, for it declares that God is known to

[2] For a definition of apparition, see Pohle-Preuss, *The Divine Trinity* (St. Louis: Herder, 1926), p. 252. For a definition of appropriation, see *ibid.*, p. 244: For a definition of generation, see *ibid.*, p. 210; of procession, *ibid.*, p. 212.

[3] I Tim. 6:3.

[4] *Ibid.*

have an offspring whom He supremely loves—the Word coequal with Himself—whom "from all eternity He begat and
in whom He has disposed of all things," [5] through whom He
has brought forth all and governs all, through whom made
flesh, God out of His great goodness redeemed man by the
most precious blood of the Word and fed him after he was
redeemed. It also says that through Him at the end of the
world, by conferring the greatest mercy, He will deliver man
from all misery so that through Christ we are all chosen sons
of the Almighty Father in whom there will be the consummation of all faithfulness, both on the part of God toward us
and vice versa.

5. In so far as faith directs what we should think of God in
the highest manner, not only does Holy Scripture bear testimony but also all creation. On this point, Augustine says in
the fifteenth book of *De Trinitate* in the fourth chapter: "Nor
does the authority of the divine books alone state that God
exists, but everything which surrounds us and with which we
are connected, the very universal nature of beings proclaims
that they have a vastly superior Creator who gave us a mind
and a natural reasoning power by means of which we judge
that living objects are to be preferred to inanimate objects,
things endowed with sensation to non-sentient things, intelligent creatures to non-intelligent, things immortal to things
mortal, things possessing potency to things impotent, things
righteous to things unjust, things well formed to things shape-
less, good to evil, things incorruptible to things corruptible,
things immutable to things mutable, the invisible to the visible, the incorporeal to the corporeal, the happy to the miserable. Through this process, since without hesitation we
place the Creator before all things created, it behooves us to
admit that He exists in the best manner, knows and understands all, to admit that He is incapable of death, corruption,
or change, that He has no body, but is a spirit, most omnipo-

5 Thus the *Glossa ordinaria* on Ps. 61:12.

tent, most righteous, most beautiful, the best, and the happiest." [6] Behold in these twelve are included the most noble qualities of the divine essence. But afterward, as Augustine himself shows,[7] these twelve qualities are reduced to three, namely, eternity, wisdom, and beatitude, and these three to one, namely, wisdom. In wisdom are included the generating mind, the generated Word, and the love joining both, and faith directs that the Blessed Trinity consists of these. Since the highest wisdom posits the Trinity, it posits also nonetheless all the above-mentioned most noble qualities, namely, unity, simplicity, and all the others that follow. It follows of necessity, then, that the noble qualities mentioned above in the divine essence are simultaneous with the Most Blessed Trinity.

CHAPTER THREE

THE UNDERSTANDING OF THIS BELIEF

1. For an understanding of this belief, sacred doctrine teaches that in the divine persons there are two emanations, three hypostases, four relations, and five notions but there are only three personal properties.

2. The explanation of this is as follows: Because the first and the highest beginning by the very fact that it is first is the simplest and by the very fact that it is the highest is the most perfect, it follows that it communicates itself in a most perfect manner because it is most perfect; it is completely indivisible by the very fact that it is most simple; and consequently without violation of the unity of nature, there are modes of emanating perfectly. The modes of emanating perfectly are only two, namely, by the mode of the nature and of the will. The

---

[6] Augustine, *De Trinitate*, XV, 4, 6.
[7] *Ibid.*, XV, 5 ff., especially 5, 7–10.

first is a generation and the second is spiration or procession, and these modes of emanation are present in the Trinity.

3. And because from two substance-producing emanations it is necessary that two hypostases emanate; it is likewise necessary to posit that the first hypostasis does not emanate from another—lest there be an infinite series. Hence there are three hypostases in the Trinity.

4. And because to any given emanation there is a double associated relation, there are four relations, namely, paternity, sonship, spiration, and procession.

5. Because by these relations the divine hypostases are made known to us, and in addition that hypostasis is made known which is the first basis of an existence from the very beginning, for it is not produced—and this is its very excellence—it follows that there are five notions, namely, the four relations indicated above, together with innascibility.

6. And because any given one of the persons has a single property by which He is chiefly made known to us, there consequently are only three personal properties which are expressed properly and principally by these names: Father, Son, and Holy Ghost.

7. Since it is proper to the Father that He be without birth and ungenerated, He is the beginning without a beginning and therefore He is the Father. Innascibility designates Him in a negative manner, and as a consequence it designates Him by the mode of position, because innascibility in the Father posits the source of fullness. The beginning without a beginning designates Him by the mode of position in a negative manner. Being the Father designates Him by the mode of position and relation, properly, completely, and determinately.

8. Similarly since the Son is the Image, the Word, and the Son, Image designates that Person as the expressed similitude, the Word as the expressive similitude, and Son as the hypostatic similitude; or in other words, Image designates the Son

as the conformed similitude, the Word as the intellectual similitude, and the Son as the similitude of the same nature.

9. In the same way, since it is proper to the Holy Ghost to
be the gift, the nexus or love of both and also the Holy Ghost,
the gift designates Him as a voluntary gift, the love or nexus as
a voluntary and especial gift, and the Holy Ghost designates
Him as a voluntary, especial, and hypostatic gift. Hence it is
that by these three names, Father, Son, and Holy Ghost, the
personal properties of the three persons are implied. These
truths we must grasp to understand the belief in the Trinity.

CHAPTER FOUR

THE CATHOLIC EXPRESSION OF THIS BELIEF

1. As to the catholic expression of this belief, we must
hold, according to the writings of the holy doctors, that in the
divine persons there are: two modes of predicating, namely,
the modes of substance and of relation; three modes of suppositing, namely, the modes of essence, of person, and of hypostasis; four modes of indicating substance, namely, by the
name of essence, of substance, of person, and of hypostasis;
five ways of speaking, namely, who [quis], how [qui], which
[quae], what [quod] and whereby [quo]; and three modes of
differentiation, namely, according to the different mode of
existence, according to the different mode of behavior, and
according to the different mode of comprehension.

2. The explanation of this is as follows: Since the first beginning is the most perfect and at the same time the most
simple, all things possessing perfection are properly and truly
said of it; hence all things having imperfection are not postu-
lated of it, or if they are, are used by assimilation to human
nature or by a process of transferring. Since there are ten

predicaments (namely, substance, quantity, relation, quality, activity, passivity, place, time, position, and habit),[8] and since the last five are properly directed to corporeal or mutable things, it follows that they are not attributed to God except in a transferred and figurative manner. The other five categories are truly attributed to God so far as they bespeak His completion and yet do not argue against the divine simplicity. All the above-mentioned categories, therefore, are that very thing about which they are predicated, and thus by a comparison with the subject in which they inhere, are all said to go over into that substance. But relation is excepted since it has a double comparison, namely, as to the subject in which it is and as to the end toward which it tends. In the first mode, it goes over lest it should give cause for a composition; in the second mode it remains that it may make a distinction. Hence it follows that "substance contains the unity, and relations make the Trinity manifold,"[9] and therefore only these two modes of predicating differences remain. And about these, the rule is given: that those modes which are stated according to substance are said about all, singly, at the same time, and individually; those which are spoken according to relation either are not spoken of all, or if they are spoken of most, are spoken plurally, as related, distinct, like, equal, all because of an intrinsic relation. Yet the term "Trinity" includes both.

3. Since many relations are capable of existence in one person, just as many persons exist in one nature, the distinction between notions does not imply a diversity of the person, and a distinction between persons does not imply a diversity of nature. On that account, not all that belongs to the essence belongs to the notion or the person, and conversely. Hence it is that there are three ways of suppositing and in this regard this rule is usually given: when essence is supposited,[10] neither

[8] Aristotle, *De praedicamentis.*

[9] Boethius, *De Trinitate,* 6.

[10] For the meaning of "supposit" at this point, cf. Alexander of Hales, *De sententiis,* Part I, q.56, n.5.

notion nor person is supposited, and when notion is supposited, neither essence nor person is supposited, and when person is supposited, neither essence nor notion is supposited as is plain from examples.

4. And because there is a true distinction in the things supposited of substance though one essence remains, it is necessary that the substance be signified in a manifold manner, namely, as communicable and incommunicable. As communicable, by the mode of the abstract through the term essence, and by the mode of the concrete through the term substance; as incommunicable either as distinguishable by the term hypostasis, or as distinct by the term person. Or also as distinct as regards quality and hence an hypostasis, or as distinct remarkably or perfectly and hence a person. Examples of these four are found in creation: humanity, man, some man, and Peter; the first bespeaks the essence, the second the substance, the third the hypostasis, and the fourth the person.

5. And because in the person who is distinguished we ought not only to consider him who is distinguished, but also the one from whom he is distinguished, and this is the property or notion, it follows necessarily that in the divine persons there are five modes of speaking in an equal manner and of inquiring, namely, who [quis] by reason of the person, how [qui] by reason of the hypostasis, because it bespeaks a thing indistinctly supposited of the substance, which [quae] by reason of the notion, what [quod] by reason of the substance, what [quid] or whereby [quo] by reason of the essence.

6. Because all these modes take their roots in the unity of essence, for whatever is in God is God Himself one and only, it follows that these modes do not posit a difference in essence or in existence. And there are only three modes of differentiation, namely, according to the modes of existence or emanation, as one person differs from another person; according to the modes of behavior as person and essence differ (because one person is compared to the other and hence is dis-

tinguished, though the essence is not compared to the other and hence is not distinguished); according to the modes of understanding, just as one substantial property differs from another, as goodness from wisdom. The first difference is greater, and this can be found in the divine persons for it is in the things supposited, so that one is not spoken about the other. The second difference is lesser because it is in the attributes, for, though one can be said about the other, as the person is about the essence, nevertheless something is said about one which is not said about the other, as: the person is distinguished and compared, the essence is not. The third difference is the least because it is in the connotations. Although one is said about the other alternately and the same thing can be said about both, nevertheless the same thing is not connoted of both and by the same thing it is not intended that both be understood. From the first mode of differentiating arises the plurality of persons, from the second mode the plurality of the substantial and relative predications, and from the third mode the plurality of the essential properties and notions, either from eternity or in time, either properly or by assimilation, either commonly or appropriately. Examples of these statements are clear. In understanding these truths, light is thrown on what we should think and how we should speak about the Trinity of the divine persons.

CHAPTER FIVE

THE UNITY OF THE DIVINE NATURE AMID THE MULTIFORMITY OF APPARITIONS

1. In the second place, divine doctrine teaches that we should hold this in regard to the plurality of apparitions: that although God is infinite, invisible, and unchangeable, nevertheless He dwells particularly in holy men, He appeared to

patriarchs and prophets, He descended from heaven, He even
sent the Son and the Holy Ghost for the salvation of the human race. Although in God there are the undivided nature,
virtue, and operation of the Trinity, yet the sending or apparition of one person is not the sending or apparition of the
other. Although there is in the Trinity the greatest equality,
nevertheless it is the function of the Father alone to send and
not to be sent. The Holy Ghost is only sent with regard to
the divine persons, unless perchance the Holy Ghost be said
to send man. The Son, however, sends or is sent, as can be
gathered from the Scriptures.

2. The explanation of this is as follows: Although the first
principle is immense and infinite, incorporeal and invisible,
eternal and immutable, yet it is the principle of things spiritual and corporeal, natural and by way of grace, and hence
it is also the principle of all things mutable, sensible, and
finite, through which it makes itself known and manifest,
though in itself it is immutable, non-sensible, and infinite.
However, God makes Himself manifest and known in general by the universality of the effects emanating from Himself, in which He is said to exist by essence, power, and
presence because He extends Himself to all things created.
He makes Himself specially known by other effects which lead
to Him in particular and because of these effects He is said to
dwell in, to appear, to descend, to be sent, and to send. To
dwell in bespeaks a spiritual effect with an acceptance on the
part of another just as it is the effect of grace to cause grace
which is Godlike and to lead back to God and to make God
possess us and be possessed by us and through this to dwell in
us. Because the effect of grace is common to all persons, it
follows that one person does not dwell in someone without
another and hence at the same time the whole Trinity.

3. To appear bespeaks a sensible effect with an expressed
significance, as the Holy Ghost has appeared as a dove.[11] And

11 John 1:32.

because, as the divine persons have been distinguished, so they are able to be signified separately both by symbols and by names, it follows that any one of the persons is able to appear by Himself and the apparition can be suitable to all, either taken together or singly. Hence, when the Holy Ghost is said to have appeared as fiery tongues [12] and as a dove, this is not because of a new bond or a particular effect, but because of the union existing between the one symbolized and the symbol which is imputed to Him in particular both as to mode and as to origin.

4. To descend refers to one of the two above effects as just beginning. God is always present in heaven with the most blessed angels because in them He always dwells and appears. However, in sinners on earth He is in a way absent as regards both grace and knowledge. It follows that when He begins to appear or dwell in, He who is present in heaven and as it were absent from us, comes to be present on earth. Hence, though He is not changed in Himself, nevertheless He is said to descend on us.

5. To be sent bespeaks the effects mentioned above coupled with eternal production. For the Father sends the Son when, by making Him present to us through knowledge or grace, He makes it known that the Son proceeds from Him [the Father]. And because the Father proceeds from no one, it follows that He is never said to be sent. Because the Son both produces and is produced, He sends and is sent. Because the Holy Ghost is eternally produced, but does not produce except in time, it is properly said of Him that He is sent, but it is not within His province to send except in regard to creatures. Hence it is apparent that the following are not proper to Him and need explanation, namely, that the Holy Ghost sends Himself, that the Holy Ghost sends the Son, that the Son sends Himself, except that it be understood that He was born of the Virgin. It is plain, then, why to send and to be sent are not applied to all

12 Acts 2:3.

persons: because, though it bespeaks an effect in the creature, it expresses an intrinsic relation such that to send bespeaks an authority, to be sent bespeaks subordination by reason of the eternal procession achieved from within.

CHAPTER SIX

THE UNITY OF THE DIVINE NATURE AMID THE MULTIPLICITY OF APPROPRIATIONS

1. In the third place, Holy Scripture directs that we should hold this in regard to the plurality of the appropriations: that, though all essential things are found in all the persons equally and without distinction, nevertheless unity is said to be appropriate to the Father, truth to the Son, and goodness to the Holy Ghost. Besides this, the second series of appropriations of Hilary is recognized, namely, "eternity in the Father, form in the Image, and utility in the Gift." [13] Besides these a third series of appropriations is recognized, namely, in the Father the reason of beginning, in the Son the reason of operation, and in the Holy Ghost the reason of finality. Besides these a fourth is recognized, namely, omnipotence in the Father, omniscience in the Son, and will or benevolence in the Holy Ghost. These, however, are said to be appropriated, not because they are proper although they always are common to all the persons, but because they lead to the understanding and knowledge of what is proper, namely, of the three persons.

2. The explanation of this is as follows: Because the principle is most noble and most perfect, the qualities of being most noble and most general are disclosed in Him in the highest degree. These however are the one, the true, and the good, which are not associated with the being's supposita but rather with its principle. One signifies a being as drawn together,

[13] Hilary, *De Trinitate*, 1.

and this obtains by the indivisibility of itself in itself. Being is true according as it is knowable, and this obtains by the inseparability of itself from its proper form. Being is good according as it is communicable, and this obtains by the inseparability of itself from its proper functioning. And because this triple undividedness follows an order for understanding so that what is true presupposes what is one, and what is good presupposes what is one and true, it follows that these qualities are attributed to the first principle in the highest degree because they are perfect and general and they are appropriate to the three persons because they are in order. It follows that the height of what is one belongs to the Father, who is the origin of the persons. The height of what is true belongs to the Son, who is from the Father as the Word. The height of what is good belongs to the Holy Ghost, who springs from both as the love and the gift.

3. And because the height of what is one is the height of what is first, for it is free from all inception, and because the height of what is true is the height of what is equal and beautiful, and because the height of what is good is the height of what is useful and profitable, there arises Hilary's second appropriation, which is: eternity in the Father, because He did not have a beginning, but is entirely the first; form in the Image, that is in the Word, because He is the height of beauty; utility in the gift, that is in the Holy Ghost, because He is the height of what is profitable and useful. Augustine explains this in other words: "in the Father, unity; in the Son, equality; in the Holy Ghost, the concord of unity and equality." [14]

4. Again, because the height of what is one and first contains the reason for the beginning and the origin, and the height of what is beautiful and splendid contains the reason for imitation and reflection; and the height of what is profitable and good contains the reason for finality, for "the good and the

---

[14] Augustine, *De doctrina christiana*, I, 5, 5.

end are the same," [15] there arises the third appropriation: of efficiency to the Father, of exemplarity to the Son, and of finality to the Holy Ghost.

5. Furthermore, because from the first and highest principle flows all power, and from the first and highest exemplar comes all knowledge, and to the final end all wishing tends,[16] it is necessary that the first principle be most omnipotent, most omniscient, and most benevolent. The first and the highest unity turning back upon itself by a complete and perfect reflection is the most omnipotent, the wisest truth, and the most benevolent goodness. These are appropriate because they imply an order. Will gives the foundation for knowledge, and will and knowledge imply power and strength because "the power to know is a certain power." [17]

This explains what the appropriations are, to whom they apply, and for what reason they exist. Nevertheless, power, wisdom, and will are most especially those appropriations in which the highest Trinity is praised in the Scriptures. Hence we should say something briefly and summarily about these.

CHAPTER SEVEN

THE OMNIPOTENCE OF GOD

1. We should hold these truths about the omnipotence of God according to Holy Scripture: that God is omnipotent in such a way that there are not attributed to Him any culpable acts such as lying and evil wishes, nor acts liable to punishment, such as fearing and sorrowing, nor corporeal or material acts, such as sleeping or walking except perhaps by simile,

[15] Aristotle, *Physics*, II, 3; *Metaphysics*, IV, 2.
[16] Aristotle, *Ethics*, I, 2.
[17] Richard of St. Victor, *De Trinitate*, VI, 15.

nor unsuitable acts, such as being able to make Himself greater
or being able to make another God equal to Himself or infinite in act and similar things, because as Anselm says: "Whatever is unsuitable even in the least degree is impossible with
God." [18] Although this unsuitability is not possible, yet He is
truly, properly, and perfectly omnipotent.

2. The explanation of this is as follows: Because the first
principle is the power of powers which is simple power, the
quantitative designation [19] added to it has reference to the
power to do certain things, and this is called simple power.
Those things exist which proceed from a complete and ordered power. I say, however, that that power is complete which
is not capable of a deficiency, of submission, or of need. Power
is lacking in the act of sinning, it submits in suffering, it includes a need in corporeal actions. The divine power, because
it is the highest and most perfect power, does not spring from
nothing, nor is it under the power of another, nor does it
need someone else. Hence it is incapable of culpability, pen-
alty, or materiality, and this is so because an omnipotent power
is a complete power.

3. Power may be spoken of as ordered in a triple sense:
according to act, according to aptitude on the part of the creature, and according to aptitude on the part of the uncreated
power alone. What is possible with regard to power in the
first way, is not only possible but also actual; what is possible
in the second way and not in the first is possible simply, though
not actually; what is possible in the third way, but not in the
first or second, is possible for God but is impossible for the
creature. What is not possible according to any of the ways
mentioned above, as is the case with that which is directly repugnant to order as regards the primordial and eternal causes
and reasons, is impossible simply, as, for instance, that God
should make something infinite in act or that He should cause

18 Anselm, *Cur Deus homo*, 20; *De fide Trinitatis*, 5.
19 Namely, the term "all" in "omnipotent."

something to exist and not exist at the same time, that He should make that which has happened not to have happened, and other things such as these, for their possibility is contrary to the order and completeness of the divine power. Thus it is clear what the divine power embraces and also what ought to be said to be possible simply and what impossible simply and that the impossibility of doing certain things is compatible with true omnipotence.

CHAPTER EIGHT

THE WISDOM, PREDESTINATION, AND FOREKNOWLEDGE OF GOD

1. With regard to the wisdom of God, we must hold these truths, namely, that divine wisdom itself most easily comprehends all things good and evil, past, present, and future, actual and possible, and in this way things incomprehensible to us and infinite. Yet this comprehension is such that the divine wisdom is in no way diversified in itself, though it gives rise to diverse names. In so far as it is capable of knowing all things possible, divine wisdom is called knowledge or cognition, in so far as it is capable of knowing all the things which happen in the universe, it is called vision, in so far as it is capable of knowing all that has a good existence, it is called approbation, in so far as it is capable of knowing those things which are in the future, it is called foreknowledge and prevision, in so far as it is capable of knowing those things which ought to be done by God Himself, it is called disposition, in so far as it is capable of knowing what things ought to be rewarded, it is called predestination, in so far as it is truly capable of knowing those things which ought to be damned, it is called reprobation.

2. Because this wisdom is not only capable of knowing but also is the reason for being able to know, it follows that in so

far as it is the reason for knowing all things known it is called light, in so far as it is the reason for knowing things seen and approved it is called a mirror, in so far as it is the reason for knowing things beforehand and their disposition it is called the exemplar, in so far as it is the reason for knowing things predestined and reprobated it is called the book of life. Hence He is the book of life in respect to things returning, the exemplar in respect to things going forth, and the mirror in respect to things happening, and the light in respect to all of these. Idea, word, art, and reason look to Him as exemplar: idea according to the act of viewing beforehand, word according to the act of proposing, art according to the act of accomplishing, reason according to the act of completing, because it adds the purposiveness of an end. Though all these things are truly one in God, one often is taken for another.

3. Though divine wisdom by reason of the diversity of things known and connoted goes under many names, yet it is not diversified in its intrinsic principle. The divine wisdom knows contingent things infallibly, mutable things immutably, future things presently, temporal things eternally, dependent things independently, created things uncreatedly, and things other than itself it knows in itself and through itself. And since it knows contingent things infallibly, liberty and changeableness of the will are compatible with predestination and foreknowledge.

4. The explanation of this is as follows: Because the first principle, by the very fact that it is first and highest, has cognition which is at the same time most simple and most perfect since, being most perfect, it knows all things most distinctly under all the conditions that things have or can have, and because it knows future things to be future and present things to be present and good things to be approved and evil things to be reprobated, it follows that a diverse list of terms is used as has been explained above.

5. But because the perfection of wisdom is compatible with

the height of simplicity, the first principle knows all things other than itself in itself and through itself. From this it follows secondly that it knows created things uncreatedly, thirdly that it knows dependent things independently, fourthly that it knows temporal things eternally, fifthly that it knows future things presently, sixthly that it knows mutable things immutably, and seventhly that it knows contingent things infallibly.

6. Thus contingent things, remaining contingent, are objects of divine wisdom infallibly, both those contingent things that are subject to nature and those that are dependent on the freedom of the human will. Thus he who wishes to understand how the freedom of the created will is compatible with the infallibility of the eternal predestination, must proceed by going from the last step through those seven steps back to the first, which is that the first principle most perfectly knows all things in itself because it is the most certain truth. From this fact other statements made above are infallibly deduced by reasoning.

7. Just as the certitude of the divine knowledge is compatible with the contingency of the things known because the divine wisdom is both most simple and most perfect, so the unity of divine knowledge is compatible with the multiformity of conceptions and ideas arising from the same cause. Because the divine knowledge is most perfect, it knows very clearly things universal and singular and represents all those things most clearly and perfectly; hence the divine knowledge is said to have conceptions and ideas of singular things and also to have the most perfectly expressed similitudes of things. Because the divine knowledge is most simple, all these similitudes are one in His knowledge. Hence, just as God by one power produced all in time according to the manifold integrity of things, so by one truth He expressed all things eternally. And just as the all-powerful active operation as regards the thing is one in the most high God though the production of things is said to be more by reason of the plurality of the products,

so the truth of the one act of intelligence in God is one although we speak of more similitudes, ideas, and concepts by reason of the plurality of the things represented, either as existing or as future or as possible. However, these concepts or ideas, though they are one truth and light and essence, are nevertheless said to be one concept or idea. Concept or idea is spoken of in regard to something outside the thing, taken from the point of view of the basis for understanding. Idea designates a representation of a thing known, which idea in reality holds existence through God, though as to the basis of understanding, it seems to bespeak something on the part of the thing known.

8. If we seek a simile in creation, it must be said that this is proper to the exemplar because, as has been said, it is simple, infinite, and most perfect. Knowing this beforehand, other things consequently become known. Because that exemplar is most simple and most perfect, it is pure act; because it is infinite and immense, it is outside all genus. Hence it is that the exemplar which is one in existence can be a similitude expressive of many things.

CHAPTER NINE

THE WILL AND PROVIDENCE OF GOD

1. We must hold these truths about the will of God: that it is so correct that it cannot in any way be turned aside, that it is so efficient that it cannot be impeded in any way, that it is such a unity that it has multiformity only by the way it is signified.

2. The divine will which is the will of His good pleasure [beneplaciti] is designated by the will of the sign according to the five different terms: precept, prohibition, counsel, fulfillment, and permission, and whatever takes place in the uni-

verse is disposed by the will of His pleasure. "The will of God is the first and highest cause of all species and motions. Nothing happens visibly or sensibly in that fullest and most immense state of all creation, which is not ordered or per- mitted by the interior, invisible, and intelligent court of the highest Commander, following the ineffable justice of rewards and punishments, graces and retributions." [20]

3. And because that will, governed by reason, is called provi- dence, all things that happen in the universe are done and governed by divine providence, which is thoroughly beyond reprehension because it lays down no precept, no prohibition, no counsel, except according to justice; it does nothing except for good, it allows nothing contrary to justice.

4. The explanation of this is as follows: The first principle, since it is the height of what is noble, both possesses a will and possesses this will in the most noble manner. Since the will of itself bespeaks that which causes a rule of correctness and an efficiency in operation to be present in beings acting with choice, it is necessary that the will of God be most correct and efficacious. Hence it is most correct because in God will and truth are the same, and it is most efficacious because in God will and strength or power are the same. And because the divine will cannot be devoid of truth, it is correct and the rule of correctness. Because the divine will can in no way lack power, it is not only efficacious but the font and source of all efficacy so that nothing can be brought about without it, noth- ing can be done contrary to it, and there is nothing by which it can be impeded.

5. Because the divine will is most upright, no one can be upright unless he is conformed to it; yet no one is able to be conformed to it unless that will is made known to him; there- fore the divine will needs to be revealed to us as the rule of uprightness. There is, however, a certain uprightness of ne- cessity, and this lies in doing good necessarily by declining

[20] Augustine, *De Trinitate,* III, 4, 9.

evil; and there is a certain uprightness of perfection, and this lies in giving something more than is due. Accordingly the rule of uprightness is made known to us by a triple sign, namely, precept, prohibition, and counsel, which designates the divine pleasure as accepting what is just because it is done in accord with the divine precept, declined according to the divine prohibition, and fulfilled according to the divine counsel. These signs are indeed infallible signs of the divine will in so far as it is the rule of uprightness.

6. Furthermore, because the divine will is most efficacious, no one can do anything at all except by its functioning and cooperation; no one is able to fall or sin unless the divine will has justly abandoned him. Accordingly there are two signs, namely, fulfillment which is the sign of the will as efficient, and permission which is the sign of the will justly abandoning men. The divine will justly abandons because it is just that it should so manage things which it has caused to exist that it should not infringe upon the laws which it has set up, but should so cooperate "with things which it has created that it may allow their own motives to drive them." [21] Hence if it allows the free will which is capable of turning to both good and evil to fall from the law of nature into evil, it does not permit this to happen unjustly.

7. Furthermore, if by grace He assists and sustains, He does no one an injury. It follows that He does act neither unjustly nor wholly on the exigency of merits because merits do not suffice in this case. Rather He acts freely and mercifully and in a certain sense justly, in so far as it satisfies the requirements of His goodness. When, therefore, He damns and reprobates, He operates according to justice, although when He predestines, He acts according to grace and mercy, which do not exclude justice. Because all men in accord with the amount of evil they have done ought to be damned, more should be reprobated than chosen so that it may be shown that salva-

[21] Augustine, *De civitate Dei*, VII, 30.

tion is in accord with a special grace but damnation is in accord with common justice. It follows that no one can complain of the divine will, because it does all things most uprightly; and we ought always to give thanks for and show honor to the guidance of divine providence. If anyone seeks to ascertain why a greater gift of grace is allotted to one sinner than to another, he should be silent and cry out with the Apostle: "O the depth of the riches of the wisdom and of the knowledge of God! How incomprehensible are His judgments and how unsearchable His ways! For who hath known the mind of the Lord? Or who hath been His counselor? Or who hath first given to Him, and recompense shall be made him? For of Him and by Him and in Him are all things; to Him be glory forever." [22]

[22] Rom. 11:33–36.

PART TWO

THE CREATION OF THE WORLD

CHAPTER ONE

THE PRODUCTION OF THE ENTIRE WORLD

1. After this brief review of the Trinity of God, some things should be said about the creation of the world. In the latter regard, we must hold these truths in brief: that the entire worldly machine was produced, as regards its existence, in time and out of nothing by a single first principle, unaided and supreme. And the power thereof, since it is tremendous, disposed of "all things in measure and number and weight." [1]

2. We must in general understand the following statements about the production of things, for by them truth is found and error refuted. When we say the world was made in time, we exclude the error of those who posit an eternal world. When we say the world was made out of nothing, we exclude the error of positing an eternity with regard to the material principle. When we say the world was made by a single principle, we exclude the error of the Manichaeans, who posit a plurality of principles. When we say that the world was made by one unaided and supreme, we exclude the error of positing that God has created lesser creatures through the ministration of intelligences. When we say the world was made "in measure and number and weight," we make it clear that the creature is the result of the Trinity creating in a triple role of causality: in the role of efficient cause from which the creature derives unity, moderation, and measure, in the role of exemplary cause from which the creature derives truth, form, and number, and in the role of final cause from which the creature derives goodness, order, and weight. All these things are found

[1] Wisd. 11:21.

49

as a vestige of the Creator in all creatures, either corporeal or spiritual or those composed of both qualities.

3. The explanation of this is as follows: Because there is a perfected order and a status in things, it is necessary that we reduce all things to one principle which is first so that it gives status to other things, and is most perfect so that it gives completion to all other things. Because the first principle in which there is status is not capable of existence except as one alone, it must, if it produces a world, produce creation out of nothing since it is not capable of producing creation from itself. And because production from nothing posits existence after nonexistence on the part of the thing produced and immensity in the productive faculty on the part of the producer, and since this resides in God alone, the creation of the world must have been accomplished in time by His own tremendous power acting in itself and immediately.

4. Furthermore, since the principle from which the perfection of the universe proceeds is most perfect, it must act from itself, according to itself, and because of itself since in none of its actions does it need anything outside itself—it must have, with regard to any given creature, the force of a threefold cause, namely, efficient, exemplary, and final; it is even necessary that every creature be related to the first cause according to this threefold condition. Every creature is constituted in being by the efficient cause, made to conform to the exemplary cause, and ordained to a purpose. Hence every creature is one, true, and good; limited, well-formed, and wellordered; measured, distinguished, and weighted. Weight is an ordered inclination. This we say in general about every creature whether corporeal or incorporeal or composed of both qualities, as is the case with human nature.

CHAPTER TWO

CORPOREAL NATURE AS REGARDS ITS BECOMING

1. We should consider corporeal nature as regards its becoming, as regards its being, and as regards its operation. We should especially hold these truths about corporeal nature as regards its becoming: that it was brought into existence in six days so that in the beginning before any day God created heaven and earth.[2] On the first day light was made, on the second the firmament was made in the midst of waters, on the third day the waters were separated from the land and gathered in one place, on the fourth day the heavens were filled with luminous bodies, on the fifth day the air and water were filled with birds and fishes, on the sixth day the earth was filled with animals and men, on the seventh day God desisted not from toil or work, for He still worked, but from the creation of new forms because He had done all things either in likeness, as is the case with things which are propagated, or in a seminal reason, as is the case with those things which are brought into existence in other ways.

2. The explanation of this is as follows: Because things flow from the first and the most perfect principle and such principle is most omnipotent, most wise, and most benevolent, it follows that things were so brought into being that in their production the triple nobility and excellence mentioned above is made manifest. And it also follows that the divine operation was triform in producing the worldly machine, consisting of creation which corresponds to omnipotence, distinction which corresponds to wisdom, and embellishment which corresponds to unbounded goodness. And because creation is from noth-

[2] Gen. 1:1.

ing, it was in the beginning before all days as the foundation of all things and of all times.

3. Further, because the distinction of the bodies of the world was accomplished in a triple way, it was done in the space of three days. There is a distinction of nature luminous from that transparent and opaque, and this was done on the first day by the division of light from darkness. There is the distinction of nature transparent [moisture] from that transparent [air], and this was done on the second day by the division of the waters from the waters. There is the distinction of nature transparent from that opaque, and this was done on the third day by the division of the waters from the earth. Among these things, however, the distinction of the celestial and the elemental should be implicitly understood, as shall afterward be pointed out.[3] Therefore the distinction ought to have taken place in the space of three days.

4. And because embellishment corresponds to distinction, it ought similarly to be finished in three days. The embellishment of the luminous nature was done on the fourth day in the formation of the stars, the sun, and the moon. The embellishment of the transparent nature was done on the fifth day on which the fishes and the birds were made from the waters for the embellishment of the water and the air. The embellishment of the opaque nature, namely, of the earth, was done on the sixth day, during which the beasts were made and the reptiles and even human nature as the consummation of all.

5. Though God was able to do all these things instantaneously, He preferred to accomplish them in a series of periods as a distinct and clear representation of power, wisdom, and goodness, because of a convenient correspondence in days or periods with His operations; and further, since in the foundation of the world the seeds of things to be done ought to be established, they were established as were the prototypes of future ages. Whence in these seven days the distinction of all

[3] Cf. *infra,* chaps 3 and 5 of this part.

the times which are explained in the course of the seven ages [4] is presented, as it were seminally. Hence to the six days of work was added a seventh day of quiet. This day is not said to have an evening, not because it did not have a succeeding night, but to indicate the rest of souls which never will have an end. If, however, it should be said in another way that all things were made together,[5] then all these seven days are referred to the angelic consideration. Yet truly the first manner of speaking is wholly consonant with Scripture and with the authority of the saints, both those who have gone before and those who have followed after St. Augustine.

CHAPTER THREE

CORPOREAL NATURE AS REGARDS ITS EXISTENCE

1. We should hold these truths about corporeal nature as regards its existence: that the whole machine of the corporeal world consists of celestial and elemental nature. The celestial nature is divided into three celestial principles, namely, the empyreum, the crystalline heaven, and the firmament. Within the firmament, which is the starry heaven, are contained the seven orbs of the seven planets which are: Saturn, Jupiter, Mars, the Sun, Venus, Mercury, and the Moon. Elemental nature is divided into four spheres, namely, fire, air, water, and earth, and thus by proceeding from the highest rim of heaven down to the very center of the earth, ten celestial orbs and four elemental spheres are found. From these the whole mechanism of the sensible world is distinctly, perfectly, and ordinately integrated and established.

2. The explanation of this is as follows: Because corporeal

4 Cf. *supra,* chap. 3 of the Prologue.
5 Ecclus. 18:1.

nature for its own perfection and the expression of the multi-form wisdom of the first principle requires a variety of forms such as appears in minerals, plants, and animals, it was necessary to establish some simple bodies which could be mingled in many ways for the production of many forms. Such is nature subject to contraries, the elemental. It was also necessary that a nature be made by which these contrary bodies might be reconciled in a mixture, and such is the nature of light and the supercelestial body.

3. And because a mixture cannot come into existence except by the action and passivity of contraries, a double opposition was necessarily created in the elements, namely, as regards the active qualities which are hot and cold, and as regards the passive qualities which are moist and dry. And because any given element acts and is acted upon, it has two qualities, one active and the other passive, and yet such that one is chief and proper. Hence there necessarily are only four elements, following the four qualities spoken of above and their quadruple combination.

4. Celestial nature either is uniform and immobile, and this is the empyreum because it is pure light; or it is mobile and multiform, and this is the firmament; or it is mobile and uniform, and this is the middle heaven between the empyreum and the starry heaven, namely, the crystalline heaven. But the fourth member, namely, that which is multiform and immobile cannot exist, because multiformity tends to a varied motion and not to a uniform quiet.

5. There are, therefore, three heavens of which the first is luminous throughout, namely, the empyreum, the second is transparent throughout, namely, the crystalline, and the third, namely, the firmament, is a combination of both. Since the three heavens are incorruptible and the four elements are variable, God so arranged the seven planets that the necessary connection, harmony, and correspondence might exist. The planets by their variety of motions and by the incorruptibility

of forms make, as it were, a certain chain and join the inferior elemental orbits and the superior celestial for the completion and embellishment of the universe. This is said to have been ordained according to a numerical proportion and the integration of the ten celestial orbs and the four elemental spheres by returning to Him proportionately as much beauty as it has perfection and order, represents in its own way the beginning.

CHAPTER FOUR

CORPOREAL NATURE AS REGARDS ITS OPERATION AND INFLUENCE

1. As regards operation, we should hold these truths about corporeal nature: namely, that the planets influence terrestrial and elemental things by introducing the distinctive division of time, namely, days, months, and years. As the Scripture says, they should be "for signs, and for seasons, and for days and years." [6] They even influence as regards the effective production of things generable and corruptible, namely, mineral, vegetative, and sensitive life and human bodies. Nevertheless they are as signs of times and have a governing effect on operations though they are not certain signs of future contingencies, nor do they exert influence upon the freedom of choice through the power of the constellation, which some philosophers say is fate.

2. The explanation of this is as follows: Since in celestial bodies, on account of their proximity to the first principle, there are light, motion, heat, and power (light by reason of their form and appearance, motion with respect to the influence from a superior body, heat with respect to the inferior nature receiving it, and power by reason of all the matters al-

[6] Gen. 1:14.

ready mentioned), since, I repeat, this is so, the celestial bodies by light and motion are responsible for the distinctions of time, namely, of the day according to the light of the sun and the motion of the firmament, of the month according to the motion of the moon in an oblique circle, of the year according to the motion of the sun in its orbit, of the ages according to the motion of the various planets, their distance and course, ascension and descension, retrogression and fixity. From all these arises the diversity in time.

3. By power and heat the heavenly bodies have an effect on the production of those things which are generated from the elements by excitation, by moving forward, by bringing together, so that in the union of contradictories, though this union is not of equals, they have an effect on mineral things; in the union less removed from equality they have an effect on vegetative things; in the union nearest to equality they have an effect on sentient things; and in the union of equals they have an effect on human bodies, which are adapted to the most noble form, the rational soul. All desire of sensitive and corporeal nature is designed and intended so that the soul, a form, existing, living, sentient, and intelligent, as if in the mode of an intelligent orbit, leads back to its beginning in which it is perfected and beatified.

4. And because through its origin the soul tends toward freedom of choice, it excels in this regard all corporeal power by its very freedom of choice. Through this all things are born to serve it, and nothing can rule it except God alone, not fate or the power of the star's position.

5. Wherefore it is unquestionably true that we are "the end of all things which exist," [7] and all corporeal matter was made for human service so that by all these things mankind may ascend to loving and praising the Creator of the universe whose providence disposes of all. This sensible machine of corporeal things is finally a certain home built by the supreme

7 Aristotle, *Physics*, II, 2.

Artificer for man until he comes to the home not made by hands, but in heaven, so that, as the soul by reason of the body and of the status merited now is on earth, so some day the body by reason of the soul and the status of the reward will be in heaven.

CHAPTER FIVE

THE MODE OF REPRESENTATION SPOKEN OF IN HOLY SCRIPTURE

1. From these words it is gathered that, as God established things ordinately as regards time and disposed them ordinately as regards location, so He governs them ordinately as regards influence, and Scripture is an orderly narrative as regards fullness of doctrine, though it does not so explicitly describe the distinction of the orbs, neither the celestial nor the elemental. It says little or nothing about the motions and powers of the superior bodies and about the intermingling of the elements and the bodies formed by the elements and, what is more, it says nothing explicitly about the creation of the higher spirits especially in so far as it describes the universe as brought into being.

2. The explanation of this is as follows: The first principle gave Himself to us as knowable both in Scripture and in creation, He manifests Himself by the book of creation as the effective principle, and by the book of Scripture as the redeeming principle, and, because the redeeming principle cannot be known except it be known as effective, it follows that Holy Scripture, though it principally deals with the works of redemption, certainly ought to deal with the work of creation in so far as it leads to a knowledge of the efficient first principle. And hence Scripture is a knowledge sublime and saving, sublime because it is a knowledge of the effective principle

which is God the Creator, saving because it is a knowledge of the redeeming principle that is Christ, the Savior and Mediator.

3. Again, because Scripture is sublime, namely, because it deals with the first principle and the Supreme Being, it does not descend to a special description of natures, motions, powers, and differences, but retains a certain generality in which things specific are implied, namely, by the description of the creation of the world as regards its disposition and influence, touching on nature luminous, opaque, and transparent with a certain generality.

4. Because the first principle with which Scripture deals has in itself the order of nature in existence, the order of wisdom in disposition, and the order of goodness in influencing so that the order of nature possesses simultaneity and equality, the order of wisdom possesses priority and posteriority, and the order of influence possesses superiority and inferiority, it follows that to distinguish the order of nature Scripture sets out the limits within which it is fitting that God should operate. Thus in the beginning before the lapse of time God brought the triple nature from non-existence to existence, whence Scripture says: "In the beginning God created heaven and earth. . . . And the Spirit of God moved over the waters." [8] Hence by the name of heaven the luminous nature is designated; by the name of earth, the opaque; by the name of water, the transparent or translucent, either subjected to contraries or elevated above them. Whence also the eternal Trinity is designated, namely, the Father in the name of God creating, the Son in the name of God the beginning, the Holy Ghost in the name of the Spirit of God. We must not understand the passage, "He that liveth forever created all things together," [9] to mean that He created all things into a total chaos about which the poets talk, for He made this triple na-

[8] Gen. 1:1 f.
[9] Ecclus. 18:1.

ture: the highest in the highest, the middle nature in the middle, and the lowest in the lowest; nor on the other hand are we to believe that He created it with a complete distinction, since heaven is perfect and the empty earth is a middle nature, as it were holding a middle place, not yet brought to a perfect distinction.

5. However, in order to suggest the order of wisdom in disposition, God determined that this triple nature was not to be distinguished and embellished at the same time, but according to the exigency of the triple nature created, the distinction was made in three days and the embellishment in another three so that as God in the beginning created a triple nature coordinate with the beginning of time, so by a succession of time in a triple measure of time, namely, in three days, He made a triple distinction of a triple nature created, and likewise in another three days He made a triple embellishment of the triple nature after it was made distinct.

6. To suggest the order of goodness in His influencing, He determined that this triple nature should be arranged in the world on a basis of under and over, as regards dignity and influence. And because the luminous has the highest beauty, the circumference ought to belong to it. Because the opaque has the least beauty, it ought to be the center, and because the transparent has a mediocre beauty, it is allotted the middle position. And because the nature of the transparent and translucent is common to the celestial and elemental natures and the luminous nature agrees with both, it is correctly said that the firmament was made in the midst of waters,[10] not because the waters above the heavens are flowing waters, cold, heavy, and corruptible, but because they are clear and incorruptible, transparent and sublimated beyond all contrariety. Thus the waters of the celestial nature and in celestial things are located together by reason of nobility of form.

7. The waters are also located together through power and

10 Gen. 1:6.

influence. Because every corporeal reason among lower things takes its law, origin, and power from celestial nature—for there are two active qualities, namely, hot and cold—and because there is something principally influencing the heaven and this is the hot, as the starry heaven by reason of its luminosity, it is fitting that something influence the cold, and this is the crystalline heaven. Just as the starry heaven, though it causes heat, is not formally hot, so also the heaven which is called aqueous or crystalline is not essentially cold. Thus it is that when the saints say that the waters there were designed to check the heat of the higher bodies and like things, we must understand them not as referring to formal predication but as referring to their effect and influence. Hence the establishment of creation follows the order mentioned above of the Creator of wisdom and of Holy Scripture because it is a sublime science.

8. Furthermore, because Scripture is the science of salvation, it does not speak about the work of the creation except with reference to the work of reparation. And because the angels are so created that, having fallen, no reparation can be made, as will appear in the following discussion,[11] Scripture is without explicit discussion of the fall of the angels and their creation, because no reparation ought to occur.

9. Because it is not consonant with the sublimity of Scripture to be completely silent about the creation of the most sublime creatures, Holy Writ describes their creation in so far as the sublime and saving science requires that, but in such a way that, taking a spiritual understanding, the whole of creation literally described, refers spiritually to the angelic and ecclesiastical hierarchy. Thus understood in a spiritual meaning, in those three natures first produced we have the angelic hierarchy under the name of heaven, the ecclesiastical under the name of earth, and grace, by which the other two are refreshed, under the name of water.

11 Cf. *infra.*, chap. 7 of this part.

10. Furthermore, by the arrangement of seven days is understood the sevenfold position of the Church in the lapse of the seven ages. Through this same sevenfold combination of days is understood the sevenfold conversion of the angels from an interest in creatures to an interest in God. Thus from what has been said above, the sufficiency and truth of Holy Scripture appear in the diverse opinions of the saints, namely, of Augustine and the others whose opinions do not contradict one another since all are the truth if correctly understood.

CHAPTER SIX

THE PRODUCTION OF THE HIGHER SPIRITS

1. As a consequence we should hold the following truths in regard to spiritual and incorporeal nature, to which the angelic nature belongs, and we should consider these problems: the creation of the higher spirits, the downfall of the demons, and the confirmation of the good angels.

2. We must understand that angels have four attributes from the very beginning of their creation: namely, a simplicity of essence; a personal distinction; memory, intelligence, and will because of a reason implanted in them; and freedom of choice for selecting good and rejecting evil. These four principal attributes have four others as concomitants, namely, strength in operation, loyalty to duty in administration, keenness in perception, and immutability after a decision for good or for evil.

3. The explanation of this is as follows: Because the first principle, by the very fact that it is first, produces all things out of nothing, it does so from nothing and through its own power. Not only ought it to have produced a substance distant from itself, namely, corporeal nature, but also a substance near itself, and this is an intellectual and incorporeal substance

which by the very fact that it is similar to God has a simplicity of nature and a personal distinction so that it is similar to God in substance, either common or individual. The angelic nature also has on its mind the image of the Trinity as to memory, intelligence, and will. It also has freedom of will so that it is similar to God as regards power either natural or selective, so that thus its natural power is stamped with the image of God, and the selective power with freedom of will. The angelic nature could not meritoriously achieve the glorious prize which makes each one happy unless it should have a free choice of will. This cannot exist unless it is in a rational substance which memory, intelligence, and will accompany. Where there is reason, however, it is necessary that there be an individual substance for that rational nature and that it be a spiritual and incorporeal substance and hence simple, lacking all quantitative dimension.

4. Such a simple substance by the very fact that it is simple is powerful in operation, and by the very fact that it is distinct in person has a distinction of duty in administration. By the fact that it is simple and powerful it has a keenness in perception, and by the very fact that it is simple and penetrating it is also possessed of a Godlike intellect. Therefore it has a stability after the choice of either good or evil. These characteristics are to be added to the general condition of the higher spirits.

CHAPTER SEVEN

THE APOSTASY OF THE DEMONS

1. These truths we should hold in regard to the apostasy of the demons: God made the angels good, intermediate between Himself the supreme good and the commutable good which is creation. He so made them that if they turned to

loving that which is above, they ascended to the position of grace and glory; but if they turned to the commutable good which is below, they fell into the evil of sin and its punishment because there is no "impropriety of sin without the propriety of justice." [12] First among the angels, Lucifer, laying presumptuous claim to a private good, sought after a private excellence and wished to be above the others. It follows that he fell with the others who were of the same mind as he. Falling, he was made impenitent, obstinate, blinded, and excluded from the contemplation of God and disordered in his operation, exerting himself with his whole spirit to the subversion of mankind by many temptations.

2. The explanation of this is as follows: Because the first principle is the supreme good, it does nothing but good and because from the good nothing proceeds except the good, whatever good is brought into existence by Him is less than the supreme good and hence cannot be the supreme good. Thus the angels were created good but not the supreme good. Yet they were capable of being perfected if they should tend to the supreme good by their own disposition.

3. Because by the free choice of the will, an angel was able to tend toward the supreme good or to turn to a private good, Lucifer, aroused by the thought of his own beauty and height to loving himself and his own private good, laid presumptuous claim to the height he had and sought to gain an excellence which he had not achieved. Through this presumption he constituted himself his own principle by that very glorying in himself, and through his claim constituted himself the supreme good for himself by finding repose in himself alone. Since, however, he himself was neither the supreme principle nor the supreme good, it was necessary that by his disordered attempt to ascend, he should fall and for the same reason all those of like mind.

4. Because "there is no impropriety of sin without the pro-

12 Cf. Augustine, *De libero arbitrio*, II, 19, 53; III, 15, 44.

priety of justice," it follows that since he fell into sin, he, together with the others who adhered to the same idea, instantly lost their supreme position, namely, the empyreum, and descended to the bottom, namely, to the misty atmosphere or inferno. Having fallen into error, he had by free choice fallen into punishment by the divine judgment. Because he had immutability after choice, he immediately became inflexible in evil and by this was blinded from the truth and disordered in operation and weakened in power. Further, his impious will and action in turning away from God were turned to the hate and envy of mankind. The penetrating power of his reason was deprived of true light and turned to deceptions by divinations and frauds. His loyalty to duty in administration was turned from true administration to tempting. His power was diminished and lessened so far as was permitted, and turned to performing wonderful things by rapid transformations which he achieves through corporeal creation. Because all these things were disordered by a will depraved by pride, he turned them all to the nourishing of his pride, seeking to be adored and worshiped by men and adored in the same manner as God. Hence it is that he does nothing but evil. Thus God is just in only permitting this for the punishment of wrongdoers and the reward of the good as will be evident in the final judgment.

CHAPTER EIGHT

THE CONFIRMATION OF THE GOOD ANGELS

1. We should hold these truths about the confirmation of the angels: that, just as the angels who turned away from God were instantly made obstinate in their impenitence, so those who turned to God were instantly strengthened in will by grace and glory, perfectly illumined in reason according to

their morning and evening knowledge, perfectly fortified in power, either for command or execution, and perfectly ordered in operation either contemplative or administrative. All this was according to a triple hierarchy, namely, the supreme, the middle, and the lowest. In the supreme hierarchy are the Thrones, Cherubim, and Seraphim, in the middle hierarchy the Dominations, Virtues, and Powers, in the lowest the Principalities, Archangels, and Angels. From this last group most are sent for ministration and assigned to the custody of men for whom they minister by purifying, illuminating, and perfecting according to the command of the will of God.

2. The explanation of this is as follows: Since the angels on account of their expressed similitude and nearness to the first and supreme principle have a Godlike intellect and immutability after consent by their freedom of choice—by supervenient divine grace they turned to the supreme good because they chose God and were equally strengthened by glory and perfected—it follows that in their will they have become stable and happy, and as regards reason they were made keen of intellect so that not only do they know things in a proper way, but even in art, and hence not only do they have an evening knowledge, but also a morning knowledge or even a day knowledge because of the plenitude and complete purity of that light as to which all creation may deservedly be called dark. As regards power, they have been perfectly fortified either for commanding or executing, whether they assume a body or not. As regards operation, they are most perfectly ordered (so that they are not even capable of being disordered) either by ascending to the contemplation of God or by descending to the ministration of men, because, since God is contemplated "face to face," [13] wherever they may be sent they proceed within God.

3. The angels are sent and operate according to the order of the hierarchies which was begun by nature and finished by

[13] I Cor. 13:12.

the glory that in stabilizing the ability of their free will to turn, illumined their keenness of intellect, ordered their loyalty to duty, and strengthened their power according to the four attributes named above.[14] Keenness of reason in contemplation either looks mainly to the veneration of the divine majesty or to understanding truth or to desiring goodness, and hence there are three orders in the first hierarchy, namely, Thrones to whom belongs reverence, Cherubim to whom wisdom, and Seraphim to whom benevolence. To perfect strength belong the power to command, the power to follow out a plan, and the power to expedite. The first is assigned to Dominations, the second to Virtues, and the third to Powers whose duty it is to ward off opposing powers. To perfect loyalty to duty are directed: ruling, revealing, and assisting. The first belongs to Principalities, the second to Archangels, and the third to Angels because, as custodians, they guard lest those standing should fall and they help those who are falling to arise again. Thus it is plain that all these qualities are found in the angels in greater or less degree as we gradually descend from the highest to the lowest. Each order, however, ought to be named for that power "which each has received more particularly as its gift." [15]

CHAPTER NINE

THE PRODUCTION OF MAN AS REGARDS HIS SPIRIT

1. After discussing corporeal and incorporeal nature, we should say something about that nature composed of both, first with regard to the mind, secondly with regard to the body, and thirdly with regard to the whole man. These truths we

[14] Cf. *supra,* chap. 6 of this part.
[15] Gregory, *Homilies,* XXXIV, 14.

should hold in accord with Holy Scripture about the rational soul: that it is an existing, living, intelligent form having freedom of choice. To be sure, the soul is a form having existence neither by itself nor from the divine nature but brought into being by God from nothing through creation. It is a form possessing life not from extrinsic nature but in itself, not a mortal life but a perpetual life. It is a form intelligent, not only a created form but also a "creating essence" [16] made to God's image in memory, intellect, and will. It is a form having freedom of choice because it is always free from coercion and was free from misery and fault in the state of innocence though not in the state of fallen nature. This freedom from coercion consists in nothing but the faculty of will and intellect which are the principal powers of the soul.

2. The explanation of this is as follows: Because the first principle is most blessed and most benevolent, by the very height of its own benevolence it communicates its own beatitude to the creature, not only to the spiritual and nearest creation, but also to corporeal and distant creation. Nevertheless, to corporeal and distant creation it communicates its beatitude mediately because "the divine law is this, that the lowest things are led to the highest through intermediaries." [17] Thus He made not only the angelic and pure spirit capable of achieving beatitude, but also the spirit joined to a body, namely, man. The rational soul is therefore a form capable of beatitude. Because gaining the reward of beatitude is not glorious unless it is merited and it does not deserve to be merited unless the will is unrestricted and free, it follows that freedom of choice ought to be given to the rational soul by the removal of coercion because it is of the nature of the will that it cannot be forced, though by fault it may be made miserable and the servant of sin.

3. Because a form capable of achieving beatitude is capable

---

[16] Anselm, *Monologium*, 13.
[17] Dionysius, *De caelesti hierarchia*, V, 4; *De ecclesiastica hierarchia*, V, 4.

of holding God in memory, intellect, and will, and this is existence in the image of the Trinity through the unity of essence and trinity of powers, it follows that the soul had to be capable of knowing God and all things and by this the soul is stamped with the image of God. And because nothing blessed can lose beatitude and nothing can be capable of beatitude unless it is incorruptible and immortal, the rational soul has to live a life immortal from its very nature.

4. Lastly, because all that derives its beatitude and immortality from another is mutable as regards a happy existence but incorruptible as regards existence, the soul neither exists by itself nor out of divine nature because it is mutable, nor is it produced by someone nor generated by nature because it is immortal and incorruptible. Thus this form cannot be brought into existence by generation because all that is naturally generable is naturally corruptible. From this it is apparent how the end of beatitude necessarily imposes on the soul itself as destined for beatitude the conditions stated above.

5. Because the soul as capable of achieving beatitude is immortal, it follows that, since it is united to a mortal body, it can be separated from that body. Hence not only is it a form but a substance [hoc aliquid]. Thus the soul is united to the body not only as a perfection but as a mover and thus the soul completes by way of essence what it likewise motivates. Because the soul not only gives existence but also life, sensation, and intelligence, it has a vegetative, sensitive, and intellectual power so that through the vegetative power it generates, nourishes, and increases: generates as regards essence, nourishes as regards quality, and increases as regards quantity. By the sensitive power it apprehends sensible things, retains what it has apprehended, combines and divides what it has retained. It apprehends by the exterior sensitive power which is divided into five parts paralleling the five principal bodies of the world (i.e., earth, water, air, fire, and quintessence).[18] It retains by

18 These five are mentioned in two of the codices.

memory; it combines and divides by the phantasy which is the first collective power. By the intellect it discerns truth, flees from evil, and seeks good: it discerns truth by the rational power, it rejects evil by the irascible power, it seeks good by the concupiscible power.

6. Because the discernment of truth is cognition, and the flight from evil and the desire for good are appetites, the whole soul is divided into the cognitive and appetitive.

7. By way of elaboration: because there is a double cognition of truth, either truth as truth or truth as good, and truth is either eternal which is above the soul or temporal which is below it, it follows that the cognitive power, namely, the intellect and reason, is so divided that the intellect resides in the speculative and practical and the reason in the superior and inferior part. But this indicates diverse functions rather than diverse powers.

8. In conclusion: because the appetite can be brought to anything in two ways, namely, according to natural instinct or according to deliberation and will, the affective power is divided into the natural will and the selective will. The latter is properly called the will. Because such a will is indifferent to either alternative, it is a free will. Because this indifference springs from full deliberation and will together, the free choice is a faculty of the reason and of the will so that, as Augustine says, it embraces all the rational powers mentioned above. He says: "When we are speaking of free choice, we are speaking not of a part of the soul but most certainly of its whole." [19] From the cooperation of these powers (of the reason, searching beyond itself, and of the will accompanying it), there arises the integrity of freedom, which is the principle of merit or demerit according as we choose good or evil.

[19] Augustine, *Hypognosticon*, V, 7.

CHAPTER TEN

THE PRODUCTION OF MAN AS REGARDS HIS BODY

1. These truths we should hold following the orthodox doctrines of faith in regard to the human body in its original state: that the body of the first man was created and formed from "the slime of the earth," [20] and yet was subject to the soul and in its own way proportionate. I say proportionate as to its equal composition, its most beautiful and multiform organization, its correctness of stature. Yet the body was subject in such a way that it was obedient and without rebellion, endowed with propagation and capable of propagation without lust. It had a vegetative nature without defect and was even immutable to any incorruptibility, and was not subject to death. Hence a place of earthly paradise with tranquil living was given to it. Woman was formed from the side of man as a consort and cooperator for immaculate propagation. The tree of life was given them for continuous vegetation and finally for perfect immutability through a perpetual immortality.

2. The explanation of this is as follows: Because the first principle was most powerful, wise, and good in production, and because He has made this manifest in all His effects in a certain way, He ought to manifest this most impressively in His last and most noble effect. Such is man, whom He produced last among all creatures so that in man He should appear most potently, and the accomplishment of the divine works should be reflected in him.

3. That the power of God might be manifest in man, He made him from natures very distant from each other, joined

---

[20] Gen. 2:7.

into one person and nature. Such are the body and soul: the former is a corporeal substance, the latter is a spiritual and incorporeal substance. These two are most distant from each other as kinds of substance.

4. That the wisdom of God might be manifested He made such a body as would have a proper proportion to the soul. Therefore, because the body is one with the soul for the accomplishing of, moving to, and tending toward beatitude above, it follows that for the body to conform to the living soul, it had a constitution not proportionate in weight and bulk, but proportionate in natural justice which disposes it for the most noble way of life. That the body might be suitable for the exercise of many powers, it had many organs with supreme elegance, ingenuity, and adaptability, as is plain in the face and in the hand, which is the organ of organs.[21] That the soul might be suitable for seeking heaven, the body had a rectitude of stature and a head above, so that corporeal rectitude might corroborate mental rectitude.

5. Lastly, that the goodness and benevolence of God might be manifest in man, He made man free from all taint or fault and free from all suffering or misery. Since the first principle is at the same time the best and the most just and, because He is the best, He ought not to have made man otherwise than good and hence innocent and upright. Because He is most just, He ought not to have inflicted suffering on one who had no sin. For this reason He made such a body with a rational soul that the body was obedient to the soul in such a way that no rebellion was there, no proneness to lust, no lack of strength, and no corruption of death. Likewise the body was so conformed to the soul that, as the soul was innocent and yet able to fall into sin, so the body was without pain and yet able to fall into suffering. Hence "the body was able to die and was able not to die." [22] It was able to be sufficient and was

---

21 Aristotle, *De anima*, III, 8.
22 Augustine, *De generatione*, VI, 25, 36.

able to have wants; it was able to obey the soul and also to put up a fight and rebellion against it.

6. And moreover in that state the body was such that there would be a seminal issue for the propagation of offspring by the participation of the female sex as a cooperator. The body was such that even though the humor, as it nourished the body, would be consumed by the action of heat, nevertheless its renewal would be accomplished through the food of the trees of Paradise, since the source of the humor would be restored or preserved by the tree of life, because the tree has this power whence, as Augustine says,[23] the tree of life is not only a food but also a sacrament. Therefore the incorruptibility and immortality of the body of Adam came principally from the soul by which it was contained and influenced, from the fine coordination of the body, which receptive of this influence acted harmoniously, from the tree of life which assisted and nourished it, and from the governance of divine providence which conserved its life from within and protected it against dangers from without.

CHAPTER ELEVEN

THE PRODUCTION OF MAN AS REGARDS THE ENTIRE COMPOSITE

1. These truths we should hold about the whole man residing in Paradise: that a double sense was given to him, an interior and an exterior—of mind and of flesh. There was given to him a double power of motion, namely, the imperative power in the will and the executive power in the body. A double good was given to him, one visible and the other invisible. A double precept was laid down, namely, that of nature and that of discipline: the precept of nature: "Increase

[23] *Ibid.*, VIII, 4, 8.

and multiply," [24] and the precept of discipline: "Of the tree of knowledge of good and evil, thou shalt not eat." [25] Side by side with these, a fourfold aid was given man, namely, reason, conscience, synderesis, and grace, which sufficiently equipped man to be able to remain good and to become better and to be able to be free from evil and to reject evil.

2. The explanation of this is as follows: The first principle made the sensible world to make Himself known so that, as it were, by a vestige and a mirror man should be led back to loving God the artificer and to praising Him. In accord with this idea there is a double book, one written within which is the eternal art and wisdom of God, and the other written without, namely, the sensible world. Since there was one creature which had a sense within for an understanding of the interior book, namely, the angel, and another which had its whole sense without, namely, the brute animal, so for the perfection of the universe there ought to be a creature with the two senses mentioned above to understand the book written within and that written without, that is, of the wisdom of God and His work. And because in Christ eternal wisdom and His work concur in one person, He is called the book "written within and without" [26] for the reparation of the world.

3. Because a movement corresponds to a given sense, there is a double movement in man: one in accord with the instinct of reason in the mind, the other in accord with the sensual instinct in the flesh. It belongs to the first to command and to the second to obey when things are in order. Whenever the reverse happens, righteousness and the control of the soul are thrown from their place.

4. Because to any given motion and sense there corresponds an appetite for something good, there has been prepared for man a double good: "one visible, the other invisible; one tem-

[24] Gen. 1:28.
[25] *Ibid.*, 2:17.
[26] Ezech. 2:9.

poral, the other eternal; one of the flesh, the other of the spirit. God gave one of these goods and promised the other so that one is possessed gratuitously, the other acquired by merit." [27]

5. Because a good is given in vain unless it is preserved, and it is promised in vain unless it can be attained, a double precept was given man: the one of nature for the keeping of the good already given, the other of discipline for the meriting of the promised good which cannot be better gained than by meritorious obedience. Obedience is meritorious whenever it follows a precept because of itself alone and not from any other cause. Such is called a precept of discipline because it is taught through itself, so great is the power of obedience which by its own merit leads to heaven and by its own contradiction throws one down to hell. That mandate was not given to man because of any need which God had for human service, but to offer a way of meriting our crown by pure and voluntary obedience.

6. Because man by reason of his defective nature, formed from nothing and unstrengthened by glory, was able to fall, the most benign God gave him four aids: two of nature and two of grace. He established a double rectitude in man's nature: one for judging correctly, and this is the rectitude of conscience; the other for desiring correctly, and this is synderesis whose part it is to murmur against evil and stimulate good. God superadded a double perfection of grace: one of grace [gratis data],[28] which is knowledge illuminating the intellect to know itself, its God, and the world which He has made for its sake; the other, a grace [gratum faciens], which is charity creating an affection for loving God above all things and one's neighbor as oneself.[29] Thus before his fall, man had natural perfections with grace superimposed. From this it is clear that

[27] Hugh of St. Victor, De sacramentis, I, 6, 6.

[28] For the meaning of gratia gratis data and gratia gratum faciens, see infra, footnote 2, page 141.

[29] Matt. 22:37, 39.

if he fell it was owing to his own fault, because he refused to obey.

CHAPTER TWELVE

THE COMPLETION AND ORDINATION OF THE FINISHED WORLD

1. From what has been said above we can gather that the creation of the world is a kind of book in which the Trinity shines forth, is represented and found as the fabricator of the universe in three modes of expression, namely, in the modes of vestige, image, and similitude, such that the reason for the vestige is found in all creatures, the reason for the image in intelligent creatures or rational spirits alone, and the reason for similitude in the Godlike only. Hence, as if by certain steplike levels, the human intellect is born to ascend by gradations to the supreme principle, which is God.

2. The explanation of this is as follows: Because all creatures have a looking back and dependency on their Creator, they are capable of a triple comparison with Him, namely, either as to the creative principle or as to the object toward which they tend or as to the indwelling gift. Every effect is related to God in the first way, every intellect in the second, and in the third every spirit, just and acceptable to God. Every effect, no matter how small its measure of light, is born to attain God through knowledge and love. Every just and holy spirit has the gift of the Holy Ghost infused into it.

3. Because a creature is not able to have God as its principle without being fashioned after Him according to unity, truth, and goodness, and cannot have God as its object without embracing Him by memory, intelligence, and will, and cannot have God as an infused gift without conforming to Him by

faith, hope, and charity, the threefold endowment, and because the first conformity is far removed from God, the second is closely related to Him, and the third is the closest in relation to Him, it follows that the first is said to be the vestige of the Trinity, the second the image, and the third the similitude.

4. There is therefore a rational spirit intermediate between the first and the last, of such a kind that it possesses the first inferiorly, the second interiorly, and the third superiorly. Hence in the state of innocence, since the image was not spoiled but made Godlike through grace, the book of creation was sufficient for man to prepare himself for beholding the light of divine wisdom, so that thus he might be wise since he saw the things of the universe in themselves and saw them in a proper way, saw them even in art according to which things have a triple existence, namely, in matter or nature proper, in created intelligence, and in the eternal art. As to these three, Scripture says: God said: Let it be made; He made it; and it was made.[30]

5. Because of this triple vision man receives a triple eye, as Hugh of St. Victor says, the eye of the flesh, the eye of reason, and the eye of contemplation: [31] the eye of the flesh by which he sees the world and those things that are in the world, the eye of reason by which he sees the soul and those things that are in the soul, the eye of contemplation by which he sees God and those things that are in God. Thus by the eye of the flesh man sees those things that are outside himself, by the eye of reason those things that are within himself, and by the eye of contemplation those things that are above himself. The eye of contemplation does not function perfectly except through glory which man loses through sin and recovers by grace and faith and the understanding of the Scriptures. By these the human mind is purified, illumined, and brought to

---

30 Gen. 1:3.
31 Hugh of St. Victor, *De sacramentis*, I, 10, 2.

the contemplation of things heavenly. Fallen man cannot attain them unless he first recognizes his own defects and darknesses. But this he does not do unless he considers the fall of human nature.

PART THREE

THE CORRUPTION OF SIN

CHAPTER ONE

THE ORIGIN OF EVIL IN GENERAL

1. After briefly establishing certain truths about the Trinity of God and the creation of the world, we now undertake a brief treatment of the corruption of sin. On this subject we must hold in summation that sin is not any kind of essence but a defect and corruption by which the mode, species, and order in the created will are corrupted. Hence the corruption of sin is opposed to good itself; it has no existence except in the good; it has no source except from the good which is the free choice of the will, and the will is neither completely evil, since it can wish good, nor completely good, since it can fall into evil.

2. The explanation of this is as follows: Since the first principle is a being from itself and not from another, it is necessary that it is a being because of itself and hence completely good, having no defect. Therefore there is not anything nor can there be anything which is the first and complete evil because the first principle bespeaks the greatest perfection, and the greatest evil bespeaks the very greatest defect. Since the first principle as the greatest and most perfect being cannot be deficient in essence or in operation, the greatest evil cannot exist, nor does something evil exist, nor can evil in any way reign. Because the first principle is omnipotent, it is able to bring good from non-existence into existence even without the prop of any matter. The first principle did this when it shaped the creature to whom it gave existence, life, intelligence, and choice, and it is fitting that the creature, since it has an existence according to the triple cause, should

have in its substance and will a mode, species, and order. The creature was born to perform its works from God, according to God, and because of God, and this according to the mode, species, and order implanted within it.

3. Because the creature is from nothing and is defective, it can withdraw from acting because of God, so that it may do something because of itself and not because of God and thus something neither from God, according to God, nor because of God. This is sin, which is the corruption of mode, species, and order. Because sin is a defect, it does not have an efficient cause but a deficient cause, namely, the defection of the created will.

4. Because corruption exists and is of the good, and all corruption exists in a corruptible thing, corruption does not exist except in the good. Whence, since free will corrupts the mode, species, and order in itself by withdrawing from the true good, all sin, in so far as it is of this kind, both exists from the will as its origin and exists in the will as its proper subject. The will does this when by its defection, mutability, and vertibility, it adheres to the commutable good, rejecting the non-deficient and incommutable good.

5. From these statements we gather that "sin is not an appetite for things evil, but a rejection of the better." [1] Hence there is in the appetite of the will a corruption of mode, species, and order, and through this "I proceed voluntarily, and if involuntarily it is not sin." [2] Understanding these matters well beforehand, the heresy of the Manichaeans in positing a greatest evil, the first principle of all evil, clearly falls. Also it is clear what the origin of evil is and what is the subject of evil.

[1] Augustine, *De natura boni,* 34 and 36.
[2] Augustine, *De vera religione,* XIV, 27.

CHAPTER TWO

THE TEMPTATION OF THE FIRST PARENTS

1. To understand how the corruption of sin came into the world, we should consider the fall of the first parent, the transmission of original sin, and the source or root of actual sin. In connection with the fall of the first parent, we ought to consider these three events: the temptation by the devil, the sin committed, and the punishment inflicted.

2. We must hold these truths about the trial of man: Since God had established man in the happiness of Paradise in two sexes, namely, male and female, the devil with envy of man assumed the shape of a serpent and attacked woman by first asking: "Why hath God commanded that you should not eat?" [3] and in the second place by assuring her: "You shall be as gods, knowing good and evil," [4] wishing by that temptation to cast down weaker woman and through her afterward to cause man's fall. And he did this with God's permission.

3. The explanation of this is as follows: As the first principle is most powerful in production, so He is most just in governing, and "hence He governs all things in such a manner as to allow them to perform and exercise their own proper movements." [5] Because man had been so created that he should achieve the reward of eternal peace through victory in battle and though God knows man can succumb to temptation, He ought to permit man to be tempted by him who knows how to tempt, is able to do it, and wishes to do it. Because the devil, who formerly had knowledge and rectitude, fell through pride and was made subtle and jealous, he wished to tempt through envy and knew he should use cunning. He

[3] Gen. 3:1.
[4] Ibid., 3:5.
[5] Augustine, De civitate Dei, VII, 30.

therefore tempted according as he was able and God permitted. Because in the temptation he assumed the form of a serpent, this came about by divine direction so that not only could Eve be ensnared by his cunning, but also the cunning of the devil in temptation might be made known to all the sons of Adam by that symbol.

4. The object of temptation was a precept of discipline and this likewise occurred by divine direction so that, whether she should be conquered or should conquer, the merit of her obedience or the demerit of her disobedience should be made known to all. That the devil began with woman is a mark of his cunning, for it is easier to cast down the weak, whence it is that the cunning of the enemy attacks the state in its weakest position.

5. Similarly the way the devil proceeded in his temptation exhibited great cunning because he proceeded by trying, by impelling, and by enticing. He undertook trying her by questions, he impelled her by assurances, and he enticed her by promises. First he questioned her as to the cause of the command so that he might lead her reason into doubt; secondly, when she hesitated, "lest perhaps we die," he assured her so that he might lead the irascible to contempt; and thirdly, he made promises so that he might lead the concupiscible to desire, and thus by these three modes draw her freedom of choice to consent, for freedom of choice is a faculty of the reason and the will, embracing the three aforementioned powers, the rational, the irascible, and the concupiscible. Considering these, the devil enticed woman through a triple desire, namely, by knowledge which corresponds to the rational desire, by excellence in the mode of God which corresponds to the irascible desire, and by sweetness of the tree which corresponds to the concupiscible desire. Thus he tempted all that was temptable in woman and through which she could be led to temptation, and this is the triple desire of the world, namely, "the concupiscence of the flesh and the concupiscence of the eyes,

and the pride of life." [6] The origin of all temptation lies in these three: the world, the flesh, and the devil.

CHAPTER THREE

THE TRANSGRESSION OF OUR FIRST PARENTS

1. We must hold these truths in regard to the offense of our first parents: that woman, yielding to the temptation of the devil, sought knowledge and excellence in the mode of God, sought to experience the sweetness of the forbidden tree, and finally succumbed to transgressing the precept. She was not content with this, and her offer of the fruit of the forbidden tree induced man, who was unwilling to restrain his pleasures, not to repulse woman but rather to consent to her evil persuasion, and man became a transgressor of the divine command by eating the fruit she offered.

2. The explanation of this is as follows: Man was given a double sense and appetite with respect to the two books and two goods by the first principle as has been stated before,[7] so that he could turn to either by reason of his freedom of choice; woman by giving ear to the suggestion of the serpent in the exterior book, did not turn back to the interior book which is evidenced by an upright decision of reason, but yielded to the sensual in the exterior book and began to negotiate for the exterior good. Because woman's power of sense did not attain the truth infallibly, her appetite began to be turned to the commutable good. Hence she desired what the devil promised and thus consented to do what he suggested. By desiring superior knowledge she was incited to pride, and thereby she was enticed to gratification of the palate, and hence she was

6 John 2:16.
7 Cf. *supra*, Part II, chap. 11.

laid low by disobedience in three ways. The first was a disobedience of her mind, the second of her senses, the third of her operation. Just as temptation beginning from the lower rises even to the highest because from listening she came through her appetite to consenting, so conversely, disorder, beginning from the superior, descends to the lowest, and she committed one sin which is the beginning of all sin in human nature and is the origin of all things evil.

3. After woman was enticed, she enticed man who similarly turned to the exterior book and the commutable good, whence by setting too great a value on the companionship of woman and the pleasure of her company, man neither desired to repulse woman nor to restrain those pleasures. Since he should have repulsed her and did not, the sin of woman is imputed to him. Because he was unwilling to restrain his pleasures by driving woman from himself, he began to love himself too much and in this way by withdrawing from the divine friendship fell into gratification of the appetite and disobedience.

4. There was therefore a transgression of the general precept by each, but in the case of each for a different reason, because not man but woman was seduced. Nevertheless, in both man and woman there was a disordering from the highest to the lowest because it began in the mind or in the reason, then spread to the senses, and lastly to the operation. Hence both were rendered prostrate by disobedience and enticed by taste because both were allured into pride, woman by seeking and desiring what she had not yet received, man by too greatly loving and setting too great a value on what he already had. Thus woman thought she would be elevated to the sublime by eating, but Adam, thinking himself something great and dear to God, thought he would be punished less severely. He had not yet experienced the vigor of the divine sternness. So both, while inordinately raising themselves above themselves, fell miserably beneath themselves from the state of innocence and grace to the state of sin and misery.

CHAPTER FOUR

THE PUNISHMENT OF OUR FIRST PARENTS

1. We must hold these truths about the punishment inflicted on our first parents: that man and woman immediately after their offense knew the punishment of rebellion and shame in the flesh and hence they made themselves aprons [8] to cover what ought not to be viewed. After the divine judgment, man incurred the punishment of labor and distress, the punishment of hunger and poverty, the punishment of death and dissolution into dust. As the Scripture says: "Cursed is the earth in thy work," etc. [9] To the woman however, a double punishment was given, since she has inflicted on her the punishment of many labors in conception, the punishment of sorrows in birth, the punishment of subjection to man in living together. Thus their sin, namely, eating of the forbidden tree, was punished rather severely though their fall had been easily accomplished.

2. The explanation of this is as follows: Since the first principle is most provident in His government and most upright in His management, there is not the least disorder in the universe, and because an offense is correctly ordered in its punishment, the shame of sin in our first parents was followed immediately by the propriety of judgment so that what was made inordinate in the fall of man from the order of nature fell immediately into the order of justice. Thus the twofold order encompasses all so that what has fallen from the one slips into the other. [10]

3. Because each parent by being proud in his mind and tasting with his body was disobedient to his superior nature,

8 Gen. 3:7.
9 Ibid., 3:17.
10 Boethius, De consolatione philosophiae, IV, 6.

the just judgment of God brought it about that their own inferior nature should be disobedient to them, and most of all those parts designed for the union of the sexes which are the members serving the procreative function. And because this situation arose not from nature but from their own offense, they blushed for shame and clothed themselves.

4. Again, because man despised the greatest pleasure and sought comfort in sensual pleasure, work and the defects of hunger and need were inflicted on him by the just judgment of God.

5. Lastly, because man chose to be separated from the good of the mind on account of the good of the flesh, the soul is unwillingly separated by the just judgment of God from its body by death and dissolution into dust. Hence, as God in accord with the order of nature gave man a body subject to his soul, capable of propagation without lust, capable of growing without defect, immutable since death would not intervene, so by the sin of man matters were so changed in the order of justice that God withdrew all the aforementioned qualities and imposed contrary qualities lest the offense remain unpunished and disordered, for divine providence ought never to allow that.

6. Because sin took its beginning from woman, her punishment was doubled. Because pride arose in her mind, she incurred subjection; because woman saw and desired the tree for its sweet taste, she incurred sorrow; finally, because she rejected the yoke of obedience, she incurred the chain and weight of many labors.

Thus it is clear by what order of divine providence many punishments were inflicted on man and double punishments on woman so that "the shame of sin might not be without the propriety of justice." [11]

[11] Augustine, *De libero arbitrio,* III, 15, 64.

CHAPTER FIVE

THE CORRUPTION OF ORIGINAL SIN

1. After the fall of our first parents, we must discuss somewhat the handing down of original sin. We must consider, first, the mode of corruption; secondly, the mode of handing down; thirdly, the mode of cure.

2. The mode in which mankind is corrupted by original sin is this. Whoever is generated by copulation is born by nature a child of wrath,[12] because he is rightly deprived of original justice. Because of the absence of original justice we incur a fourfold punishment as regards the soul, namely, weakness, ignorance, perversity, and concupiscence. These four were inflicted because of original sin, and these truly spiritual punishments have as concomitants in the body many punishments, defects, labors, sicknesses, and sorrows. Finally, to these punishments are added the punishment of death and dissolution into dust, the punishment of being deprived of the sight of God and the loss of heavenly glory, affecting both adults and children who are unbaptized. The children are punished along with the others but by the mildest punishment because they deserve only the punishment of those who are lost but not the punishment of the senses.

3. The explanation of this is as follows: Since the first principle accomplishes all things from Himself, according to Himself, and because of Himself, He is necessarily the best and most righteous and hence most loving and most just, and hence it is that "all the ways of the Lord are mercy and truth" [13] or judgment. If God had made man in such miseries from the beginning, He would have violated His own love and justice by oppressing man with such miseries with-

12 Eph. 2:3.
13 Ps. 24:10.

out a preceding fault. Similarly, if He later should burden us with such miseries or permit us to be so burdened without fault on our part, divine providence would govern us neither lovingly nor justly. If it is certain that the first principle is most upright and clement in creation and providence, He necessarily made mankind in such a way that in the beginning there was neither fault nor misery in man. Also, He necessarily governs mankind in such a way that He does not allow misery to exist in us unless there is some antecedent offense. Since it is most certain that we derive the many miseries of punishment from our origin, it is certain that we are all born by nature children of wrath and hence deprived of the rectitude of original justice. This privation we call original sin.

4. Because all sin bespeaks a withdrawal from the immutable good and pursuit of the changeable good, and withdrawal from the immutable good is withdrawal from the highest excellence, truth, and goodness, and pursuit of the changeable good consists in placing a greater than fitting emphasis on that good through love of it, it follows that by the loss of original justice man incurred weakness, ignorance, perversity, and concupiscence.

5. Again, because by deserting the immutable for the changeable good, one becomes unworthy of either, it follows that, because of the loss of original justice, the soul loses the temporal submission of the body by manifold corruption and death, and finally is removed from the sight of eternal light by losing the happiness of glory both in the soul and in the body.

6. Lastly, because the lack of that justice in those who are now born is not the result of any choice of their own will or of any actual delectation, it is not fitting that there should be a punishment of the senses in hell after this life for original sin because divine justice which is always accompanied by an overflowing mercy punishes us not beyond what is merited but rather short of that. We must believe that blessed Augus-

tine knew this [14] though his words on the surface seem to sound otherwise because of contempt for the Pelagian error which granted them a different kind of happiness. So that Augustine might lead them back to a middle position, he turned more easily to the other extreme.

CHAPTER SIX

THE TRANSMISSION OF ORIGINAL SIN

1. The manner of transmission of original sin is this: Though the soul does not derive its existence from the one handing down the original fault, yet the fault generated by the mediation of the flesh through concupiscence does pass down from the soul of Adam to the souls of posterity so that, as the flesh of Adam was infected by the sinning soul inclined to lust, so the flesh sown in lust and bearing with it the deadly disease, infects and corrupts our soul. This infection in the soul is not only a punishment but also a fault. Thus the person corrupts the nature, and the corrupted nature corrupts the person,[15] but divine justice is preserved in all, though the infection of the soul cannot be imputed to divine justice even though by creation it infused the soul and by infusion it united the soul to the infected body.

2. The explanation of this is as follows: Since the first principle made man in His own image as an expression of Himself, He so made man's body that all men are propagated from the first man as from one rootlike principle; He so made man's soul that, because of the express likeness to God in essence and existence and in intelligence and love, all rational spirits emanate immediately from God Himself as the first and immediate principle. And, because the spirit with its greater ex-

---

[14] Augustine, *Liber de fide ad Petrum*, 3, 36; 27, 70.
[15] Cf. Anselm, *De conceptu virginis et originali peccato*, 23.

cellence more closely resembles the first principle, God so made man that the soul should be pre-eminent to the body and the body subordinated to the created spirit as long as man obeyed the uncreated Spirit. Conversely, if the spirit should not obey God, by the just judgment of God man's body would begin to rebel against him. This happened when Adam sinned.

3. If Adam had remained firm, his body would have been obedient to his spirit and he would have transmitted such a body to posterity and God would have infused a soul into it so that, united to a body immortal and obedient to it, the soul should have the order of justice and immunity from all punishment. Correspondingly, because Adam sinned and his flesh was made rebellious to his spirit, it is fitting that he should transmit such a body to posterity and that God should infuse a soul according to His excellent plan, and the soul, since it is united to the rebellious flesh, incurred the loss of the order of natural justice by which it ought to have command over all things inferior. And because the soul is united to the flesh, it is fitting that the soul should influence the body or be influenced by the body. Because the soul cannot influence the body which is rebellious, it is necessary that it should be influenced by the body and it should incur the malady of concupiscence. Thus it simultaneously incurred the loss of justice belonging to it and the malady of concupiscence, from both of which, as Augustine and Anselm state, namely, by an aversion and a conversion, original sin is constituted.

4. Since it is most ordinate that human nature should be so created and that having been so created it should be so propagated and that it should be so punished for sin as we previously described,[16] so that the order of wisdom is served in creation, the order of nature in propagation, and the order of justice in punishment, it is clear that it is not contrary to divine justice if this sin is transmitted to posterity.

16 Cf. this chapter and the preceding chapters and chapter 11 of Part II.

5. Because original sin cannot be transfused into the soul unless the punishment of rebellion in the flesh precedes it, and that punishment does not exist unless sin precedes it, and sin does not proceed from an ordered will but rather from a disordered will and hence not from the divine will but from the human will, it is plain that the transmission of original sin is owing to the sin of the first man and not to God, not owing to established nature but to a deliberate sin. Hence it is true that, as Augustine says,[17] "propagation does not transmit original sin to posterity, but lust does."

CHAPTER SEVEN

THE CURE OF ORIGINAL SIN

1. Finally, the mode of the cure of original sin is this: that the sin is so cured that temporal punishment remains, as we see in baptized children; the sin is so cured as regards the stain of eternal punishment that it remains as to the act and motion of concupiscence; the sin is so cured in the parent that, although he is cured by baptism, yet original sin is transmitted to the offspring; the stain of original sin is so removed that the aftermath remains, and against this we ought to fight as long as we live in this world because concupiscence is not completely eliminated in anyone by ordinary grace. I make this statement since, because of a singular grace, concupiscence was never present in the most Blessed Virgin in the conception of the Son of God.

2. The explanation of this is as follows: As the infection spreads to all from the created principle from which the propagation of our bodies springs and this is from the inferior part, the flesh, so the healing, since it comes from the uncreated principle by whom souls are infused, begins with the

[17] Rather, Fulgentius, *De fide ad Petrum*, II, 16.

superior part, the soul. Because there is a distinction between men as to their souls so that one is not propagated from another as regards the soul but proceeds immediately from God, the curing grace infused in our soul by God descends on everyone in so far as he is a single person or individual but not in so far as he is a person propagating according to the power of nature. Because original sin is a malady infecting both the person and his nature, the person in the will and his nature in the flesh, the original stain is cured in the soul but the infection and the consequences remain in the flesh.

3. And because man generates not as regards what is cured in the soul but as regards what is corrupted in the flesh, not as regards the spiritual but as regards the carnal, it follows that, although one is baptized and thus is cleansed from original sin in himself, yet he transmits it to his offspring.

4. Again, because the guilt that merits eternal punishment regards a deformity of mind and person, whereas motion regards an inclination of the flesh and nature, the guilt of original sin is removed through baptism, but the consequences remain.

5. Lastly, because temporal affliction concerns the condition with regard to the flesh since the flesh remains always subject to suffering, it follows that, as the liability to suffering and corruption is not removed from the flesh through grace, the consequences (concupiscence and weakness of the body's members) are able to coexist with curative grace. Hence, though concupiscence is gradually reduced, yet, because the root is not removed, it is never altogether absent in the wayfarer except in the most Blessed Virgin through a singular grace. Because the Virgin conceived Him who was the expiation of all sin, there was given to her a singular grace by which all concupiscence was uprooted from her so that the conception of the Son of God was free from any guilt or corruption of sin. "Namely, it was fitting that the Virgin should stand out by her purity, for one more pure could not be conceived

except God. To her God the Father chose to so give His only Son who was born of His own heart, equal to Himself, and whom He loved as Himself, that the Son should be one and the same, the Son both of God the Father and of the Virgin. The Son Himself chose to make her His mother in substance, and the Holy Ghost wished and was willing to bring it about that the Son from whom the Holy Ghost Himself proceeded should be conceived and born of the Virgin." [18]

CHAPTER EIGHT

THE ORIGIN OF ACTUAL SIN

1. After a consideration of the transmission of original sin, we must consider to some extent the origin of actual sin. In regard to the source we must hold these truths in summation: that actual sin finds its origin in everyone's free will by suggestion, entertainment, consent, and action; according to James in the first chapter of his epistle, "But every man is tempted by his own concupiscence, being drawn away and allured. Then, when concupiscence hath conceived, it bringeth forth sin. But sin, when it is completed, begetteth death." [19] If suggestion and entertainment exist without consent, there is venial sin. If consent follows and the deed involves those matters forbidden by divine law, a mortal sin is committed. If the matter rests in a middle mode so that there is consent without the act or one wishes to proceed to action but is unable to do so, then the will is frustrated by the fact but is not less guilty than if it realized the action. Or if one does not wish to proceed to action but wishes to take an interior enjoyment, then it is analogous to the woman enjoying eating the fruit, and not man. It is considered among mortal sins

18 Anselm, *op. cit.*, 18.
19 Jas. 1:14 f.

though the sin be not fully completed because, by the woman's eating, the whole of mankind deserves damnation. This must be particularly understood in the case of carnal sins.

2. The explanation of this is as follows: Since sin bespeaks a withdrawal of the will from the first principle inasmuch as the will is designed to be directed from itself, according to itself, and because of itself, all sin is a disordering of the mind or the will upon which hinges the existence of virtue and sin. Actual sin therefore is an actual disordering of the will. That disordering may be either such that it destroys the order of justice and is called mortal sin because it is calculated to kill life by separating the soul from God through whom a just soul derives life, or the disordering may be of so modified a kind that it does not destroy that order but disturbs it in some way, and this is called venial sin because we are able to gain forgiveness quickly because grace is not removed nor is divine enmity incurred. The order of justice is that the immutable good is to be preferred to the changeable good, that the pure good is to be preferred to the useful, that the will of God is to be preferred to one's own will, and that the judgment of an upright reason takes precedence over sensuality. Because the law of God requires such an order and rejects its opposite, when the variable good is preferred to the pure good and our will is preferred to the divine will and the sensual appetite is preferred to upright reason, a mortal sin is committed. Ambrose says that mortal sin is a "betrayal of the divine law and disobedience of heavenly commands." [20] Mortal sin is committed either by the omission of what the divine law demands or by doing what it prohibits. And this gives rise to a double genus of sin, omission and commission.

3. When the variable good is sought unduly but is not preferred to the immutable, and utility is not preferred to purity, and our will is loved unduly, yet not preferred to the divine

[20] Ambrose, *Liber de paradiso*, VIII, 39.

will, and the flesh is desired but is not preferred to the judgment of right reason, then the sin is not mortal but venial because, though it is outside of the law it is not directly contrary to the law. The sensual appetite is not preferred to right reason unless reason consents to it, and hence mortal sin is not committed when consent is lacking.

4. If sensuality is aroused inordinately, since that inordination inclines toward evil even though the reason does not consent, there is some kind of sin because in a certain way it offends the order of justice. And because in the state of innocence sensuality is not aroused except in accord with a dictate of reason, as long as man retained that state there could not be venial sin. Now, however, because sensuality is opposed to reason whether we may wish it or not, necessarily we commit some venial sins in our spontaneous actions. Though venial sins can be prevented in particular and individual cases, they cannot be completely avoided, because they are sins and they are punishments of sin and hence they are rightly called venial because they are deserving of forgiveness [venia].

5. Because reason is not required to consent first for it to be a venial sin, if in fact consent follows after the feeling of enjoyment, there is full consent and the sin is completed because the sin was placed squarely before man, that is the highest part of his reason on which the fullness of consent hinges.

6. Because there is consent not only in the action but also in the entertainment in that the lower part follows sensuality, therefore if in sensual entertainment the reason succumbs to sensuality, the woman obeys the serpent and there arises a subversion of right order and thus a subversion of justice. Hence a mortal sin is committed though it is less serious and it is imputed not only to woman but to man by whom woman ought to be strengthened and held in check lest she obey the serpent. Thus it is clear that in the perpetration of all actual sin there is a certain imitation of the first sin according to the

explanation of the distinguished Doctor Augustine, in the twelfth chapter of *De Trinitate*.[21]

CHAPTER NINE

THE ORIGIN AND DISTINCTION OF THE CAPITAL SINS

1. We come now to an examination of the source of sins in particular, among which are certain capital sins, certain sins which are a punishment [*peccata poenalia*], and certain final or irremissible sins, corresponding to first, middle, and last.

We must hold this in brief about the origin of capital sins: that there is one beginning of actual sins, a double root, a triple fomentation, and a sevenfold head or capital sin. There is one beginning, namely, pride, about which it is written that [22] "pride is the beginning of all sin." There is a double root, namely, fear badly cringing and love badly seeking. There is a threefold fomentation, namely, the three that are in the world: concupiscence of the flesh, concupiscence of the eyes, and the pride of life. There is a sevenfold head, namely, pride, envy, anger, sloth, avarice, gluttony, and lust. Among these the first five are sins of the spirit; the last two, of the flesh.

2. The explanation of this is as follows: Because contempt for the first principle is pride since mortal sin is an actual withdrawal from the first principle, and withdrawal from the first principle cannot take place without a contempt for it either for itself or for its precept, hence all mortal sin or offense necessarily takes its beginning in pride.

3. Since no one hates the highest principle or its precept in itself unless it be because he wishes to acquire or fears to

21 Augustine, *De Trinitate*, XII, 17 ff.
22 Ecclus. 10:15.

lose something other than the first principle, all actual sin necessarily has its origin in a twofold root, namely, fear and love, which are the roots of things evil although they are not equally first.

4. All fear springs from love. No one fears the loss of anything unless he loves its possession. Hence fear has to be fomented by those things through which both fear and love are fomented. Love is inordinate with regard to the commutable good. Because that love is threefold: namely, interior in a love of superiority, exterior in a love of money, and inferior in licentiousness of the flesh, there necessarily are three radical fomentations of actual sin as mentioned above; and when the soul turns inordinately to them, all actual sins arise.

5. And because this happens in a sevenfold mode, the capital sins are seven, and the whole array of sins springs from them. Our will is disordered either because it seeks what should not be sought or because it flees what should not be fled. If the will is disordered because it seeks what is not to be sought as a present good either a commutable or an apparent good, it is either interior, and thus there is private superiority which pride desires, or it is exterior, and thus there is a sufficiency which avarice desires, or it is inferior, and thus it is either pleasurable because it leads to the preservation of the individual and thus is nourishment which is pleasurable to the taste and is sought by the glutton, or because it leads to the preservation of the species and thus it is procreation which is pleasurable with reference to touch and is sought by lust. If, however, the will is disordered because it flees what is not to be fled, it can be disordered in three ways, following a triple mode of flight. Either it flees in accord with a perverse impulse of the reason and thus is envy, or in accord with an impulse of the irascible and thus is anger, or in accord with an impulse of the concupiscible and thus is sloth. Hence four are largely appetitive and three are forces whose impulse is flight. Thus there are seven capital sins.

6. Since the experience of a thing sought after is bound up with pleasure and the experience of a thing fled from is bound up with sorrow, it follows that four have a concurrent joy and the other three have a concurrent sorrow and punishment. But all are called capital sins because they are the chief inordinations and the heads influencing in their own way many other inordinations. Hence, though certain of them look chiefly to flight, they still have their own pleasures. Envy seeks to have a good for oneself without a companion sharing in it, to have it completely. Anger seeks a good without a contrary, to have it imperturbably. Sloth seeks to have the good without some work, to have it without fatigue. Because these sins do not exist without their difficulty, they bring along with them a great army of sins directed to seeking or declining. Hence they are called capital sins, as it were heads from which all the many others flow.

CHAPTER TEN

THE ORIGIN AND QUALITY OF SINS WHICH ARE A PUNISHMENT

1. We must hold these truths about sins which are a punishment [*peccata poenalia*]: that though the evil of guilt and the evil of punishment are different kinds of evils, some are sins in that they are a punishment for sin. In a special sense those sins which have sorrow and sadness attached to them, namely, envy, sloth, and the like, are said to be sins and the punishments of sin. In a less special sense, the same is true of sins which have either a true privation of nature or shame attached to them, namely, those where the sinner is said to be given up to a reprobate sense.[23] Generally speaking, all sins that happen "between the first apostasy and the ultimate pun-

---

[23] Rom. 1:28.

ishment of hell, are rightly called sins and punishment of sin"; [24] for, as Gregory says,[25] crimes are punished by crimes. Though the same thing is called sin and the punishment for sin, we must hold that all punishment in so far as it is punishment is just and comes from God. No fault is just or from God; it comes only from the free choice of the will. Punishment which is mere punishment is inflicted by God; punishment which consists in a new fault is not from God but is contracted by us and comes from us.

2. The explanation of this is as follows: Although evil bespeaks a withdrawal from the first principle in that it injures the good, it cannot injure good except by taking something away from good, and good consists in mode, species, and order; there is no evil which is not a corruption of the mode, species, and order. Order is twofold, namely, the order of nature and the order of justice. The order of nature is in the natural good; the order of justice is in the moral good. Because the natural good is in all nature, the moral good must exist in the will. Hence the order of nature is in all nature; the order of justice exists in the elective will. Because the will "is an instrument moving itself," [26] and nature certainly is not this, it follows that the order of justice is not only a caused order but also a causing order; but the order of nature is a caused order. Because evil can disrupt the order of justice and the order of nature, there is a twofold evil, namely, of fault and of punishment.

3. Because the order of justice is a voluntary order, "the evil of fault is a voluntary disposition; the evil of punishment is an involuntary disposition." [27]

4. Lastly, because the order of justice, which is in the will, is a causing order, "the evil of fault which is the privation of order is an evil which we cause, and the evil of punishment

24 Augustine, *Enarratio in Ps.*, LVII, 9, 18.
25 Rather, Augustine, *I Contra adversarium legis et prophetarum*, 24, 51.
26 Anselm, *De concordantia gratiae et liberi arbitrii*, q.3, c. 11.
27 Augustine, *De libero arbitrio*, III, 9, 26.

is an evil which we suffer." [28] And because passion does not exist unless action naturally precedes it, nor is there an action without some succeeding passion,[29] there is no punishment without the preceding cause of fault, and no fault without some punishment accompanying it.

5. Because what we do springs from ourselves, but what we suffer can spring from ourselves and from others, namely, a superior or inferior cause, hence, though all fault springs from ourselves, not all punishment springs from us: some is caused by us, some is inflicted, some is contracted.

6. Because it is just that he who does what he ought not to do should suffer what is due him, all punishment in so far as it is punishment is just and comes from divine providence because punishment is designed for fault and creates order in that fault.

7. Because passion can come about through a removal of the natural good or of the moral good with the natural, some punishment is merely punishment, and some is a punishment and fault. This is so because the moral good which is justice is not removed except by injustice which is fault. Hence the first punishment is from God in so far as it is punishment and exists; it is from God, I say, not as institutor but as vindicator. The second punishment, since it is a fault, in so far as it has existence does not come from God but only as regards its order. Punishment either is merited if it follows on actual sin or is contracted if it follows on original sin.

8. If punishment is properly understood as an evil, in so far as it is a privation of the natural good, an involuntary condition and an evil which we suffer, it does not coincide with the evil of fault in the same thing, though it may be annexed to the same thing. If, however, we understand punishment in a larger sense so that that is said to be an evil which we suffer

---

[28] Gilbert de la Porrée, *De sex principiis,* chap. "De actione."
[29] *Ibid.*

either from ourselves or otherwise, either in nature or in will, then both coincide in the same thing but not for the same thing or according to the same thing because what is a fault in itself is called a punishment of what precedes, or what is a fault by reason of action is said to be a punishment by reason of passion. Hence it is clear how, to what extent, and in what regard a thing is said to be at the same time a sin and a punishment for sin.

CHAPTER ELEVEN

THE ORIGIN OF FINAL SINS WHICH ARE SINS AGAINST THE HOLY GHOST

1. We must hold these truths about final or irremissible sins, and these are sins against the Holy Ghost: though all sin generally is against God, triune and one, yet we can appropriately speak of some sin as being against the Father, some against the Son, and some against the Holy Ghost. Sins against the Holy Ghost are said to be irremissible in this world and in the next,[30] not because they cannot be forgiven in this world, but because they are rarely forgiven in this world as regards guilt but modified and it is as if no rescission were possible in the world to come as regards punishment. There are six different kinds of final sins, namely, a hate of the fraternal grace, rejection of acknowledged truth, despair, presumption, obstinacy of the mind, and final impenitence.

2. The explanation of this is as follows: Since sin bespeaks a withdrawal from the first principle, triune and one, all sin deforms the image of the Trinity and defiles the soul with respect to its threefold power, namely, the irascible, the rational, and the concupiscible. All sin proceeds from the free

---

[30] Matt. 12:32.

will which bears the imprint of the Trinity: of the Father because of its power, of the Son because of the reason, and of the Holy Ghost because of the will.

3. Though these three concur in all guilt, any one of them by defect in it may be the reason for disordering the others. The defect of power is impotency; of reason, ignorance; of will, perversity. Hence, since certain sins arise from impotency, others from ignorance, and others from perversity, and power is referred to the Father, wisdom to the Son, and will to the Holy Ghost, certain sins are said to be against the Father, others against the Son, and others against the Holy Ghost. Because there is nothing greater in the will than the will itself, and the will itself is the origin of sin, no sin is to such a degree voluntary and truly sin as that which arises from a corruption in the will. Since we can speak of involuntary sin in two ways, namely, owing to force and owing to ignorance (the first by a defect of power, the second by a defect of knowledge), it follows that the will alone by its own corruption, though it can resist and know a thing is evil, can choose that thing. Then it is said to sin from hardened perversity, and such a sin truly proceeds from an improbity of free choice and directly opposes the grace of the Holy Ghost. And because it really proceeds from freedom of choice, it does not have the color of an excuse, and hence there ought to be only a little or, as it were, no relaxation of the punishment due. Because it directly opposes the grace of the Holy Ghost from whom comes remission for sins, it is said to be irremissible not because it cannot be forgiven but because, in so far as it is from itself, it is directly repugnant to the medicine and remedy by which remission of sin is accomplished.

4. And because the remission of sin has to be accomplished by God through penitential grace within the ecclesiastical unity, differences in the kind of sin arise as the sin directly opposes those three. Either such sins oppose penitential grace in itself, or God by whom such grace is given, or the unity of

the Church. Thus, since the unity of the Church consists in faith and charity or in grace and truth, there is a twofold sin, namely, a hate of the fraternal grace and a rejection of acknowledged truth. If the sin is against God as the giver, since all His ways as regards justification are mercy and truth, there is a double sin: namely, one which opposes mercy, and this is despair; the other which opposes justice, and this is the presumption of impunity. If the sin opposes penitential grace in itself or according to itself, it is twofold because penitential grace makes one recoil from sins committed and guard against what may be committed. A sin against the first is obstinacy of the mind, against the second is final impenitence and accordingly final impenitence is called the state of not intending repentance. This is the species of sin against the Holy Ghost. In so far as final impenitence bespeaks a continuation of sin to the very end, it is the aftermath of all mortal sins which are not forgiven in this life and most of all the aftermath of all species of sins against the Holy Ghost.

5. Thus all sin takes its beginning in pride and has its consummation or end in final impenitence, and he who achieves this perishes in hell from which no one sinning mortally can be freed except by the intervention of the grace of the mediator Christ.[31] Thus universal salvation required His incarnation. And to Him our Lord mediator "be honor and glory forever and ever. Amen."[32]

[31] This is an exact translation of the text. Some editions here insert a phrase indicating that the intervention of the grace of Christ must take place while the sinner is still alive.

[32] I Tim. 1:17.

PART FOUR

THE INCARNATION OF THE WORD

CHAPTER ONE

THE REASON WHY THE WORD OF GOD OUGHT TO BE INCARNATE

1. After certain statements given above about the Trinity of God, the creation of the world, and the corruption of sin, we turn now to a brief discussion of the incarnation of the Word. Through the Word incarnate, the salvation and redemption of mankind was achieved, not because God could not have saved or freed mankind otherwise, but because no other way was so congruous and fitting for the Redeemer, the redeemed, and the redemptive process.

2. The explanation of this is as follows: Because the effective principle of things could not be and ought not to be anything other than God and because it is surely as important to redeem created things as to create them, just as it is as important to have a good existence as to have a simple existence, it was most fitting that the redeeming principle of things be God the most high so that, just as God created all things through the uncreated Word, so He cures all things through the Word incarnate. Because God made all things effectively, wisely, and best or benevolently, it was fitting that He should so redeem them that He might show His power, wisdom, and benevolence. What shows more power than to join in one person extremes most widely separated? What shows more wisdom and congruity than that for the perfection of the whole universe there should be a union of first and last, namely, of the Word of God, which is the principle of all, and of human nature, which was the last of all creatures? What shows greater benevolence than that God should assume the form of that

to be saved because of the salvation of that to be saved? Certainly there is shown here such benignity that nothing more clement, more benign, more amicable can be thought of. It is most fitting, therefore, that this should be the way of God the Redeemer because it demonstrates the divine power, wisdom, and benevolence.

3. Because man when he fell into sin turned away and withdrew himself from the most powerful, wise, and benevolent principle, he was made corrupt in infirmity, ignorance, and perversity, and the result is precedence of the carnal, animal, and sensual over the spiritual. Hence man was unsuited for imitating divine virtue, for learning of its light, for choosing its goodness. So that man might be redeemed from that state, it was most fitting that the first principle should descend to him by rendering Himself knowable, lovable, and imitable. Because carnal, animal, and sensual man did not know or love or follow anything except what was proportioned and adapted to his state, "the Word was made flesh"[1] for the rescue of man from this state so that God could be known, loved, and imitated by man who was flesh and in this way, by knowing, loving, and imitating, man might be cured of the sickness of sin.

4. Lastly, because man could not be perfectly redeemed unless he regained innocence of mind, the friendship of God and his own excellence by which he was second only to God, and this could be achieved only through God in the form of that to be saved, it was fitting that the Word should become incarnate. Man could not regain his excellence unless the Redeemer was God for, if the redeemed were a mere creature, then man would be subject to that mere creature and thus would not regain the state of excellence. Moreover, man could not recover the friendship of God except by a suitable mediator who could place His hand in either or both natures as conforming to and a friend of both. Hence, just as the Re-

[1] John 1:14.

deemer is like God through His divinity, so He is like man through His humanity. Man could not recover his innocence of mind except by the forgiveness of sin, and it was not fitting for divine justice to forgive sin except after a condign satisfaction for that sin. Because man could not make satisfaction for sin unless God did so for the whole of mankind and it was suitable only if man who had sinned should do so, it was most appropriate that mankind be redeemed by the God-man born of Adam's kind. Because excellence could not be recovered except by a most excellent Redeemer, nor could friendship be regained except by a most amiable mediator, nor could innocence be regained except by a most adequate satisfier, and there is no most excellent Redeemer except God, no most amiable mediator except man, no most adequate satisfier except one equally God and man, the incarnation of the Word was most congruous with our redemption. Just as mankind came into being through the uncreated Word and fell into sin by abandoning the inspired Word, so it should rise from sin through the incarnate Word.

CHAPTER TWO

THE INCARNATION: THE UNION OF NATURES

1. We ought to consider three points about the incarnate Word, namely, the union of natures, the plenitude of gifts, and the suffering of the Passion for the redemption of mankind. In regard to the union of natures we should consider these three points in order to understand the mystery of the Incarnation, namely, its operation, mode, and time.

2. According to Christian faith, we should hold these truths in regard to the operation of the Incarnation: that the Incarnation is the operation of the Trinity through whom the assumption of flesh by the Deity and the union of the Deity

with the flesh occurred in such a way that the assumption involves not only a sensible flesh but also a rational spirit with
its vegetative, sensitive, and intellectual powers, and also in
such a way that there is union not in the unity of nature but
of person, not of a human person but of a divine person, not
of the assumed but of the assuming, not of any person but of
the person of the Word alone. Such is the union that whatever
is said of the Son of God, may be said of the Son of man, and
conversely, with the exception of those terms in which the
union of the divine and human is expressed or absence [of
human personality] is implied.

3. The explanation of this is as follows: The operation of
the Incarnation proceeds from the first principle not only in
so far as it is effective but also in so far as it repairs by redeeming, satisfying, and conciliating. Because the Incarnation, in so far as it bespeaks a certain effect, stems from the
first principle, which accomplishes all things by reason of its
highest power and substance, power and operation are united
and completely undivided in the three persons, hence it must
be that the operation of the Incarnation flowed from the whole
Trinity.

4. Because the Incarnation is from the first principle in so
far as it repairs by redeeming and because all mankind has
fallen and sinned in soul and body, the entire nature must
be assumed so that all of it may be cured. And because the
carnal part is better known to us and more removed from
God, the operation should not be called an animation but
rather an incarnation so that the selection of this method
might be made clearer and a greater humiliation shown and
a more profound dignity demonstrated.

5. Again, because the Incarnation is from the first principle
in so far as it repairs by satisfying, and there is no satisfaction
except when made by him who ought to make it and can
make it, and no one ought to make it but man and no one can
make it but God, it was fitting that in the satisfaction there

be a concourse of both natures, namely, divine and human. And because it is impossible that divine nature should coincide with another nature as a part of a third nature and it is impossible that the divine nature go over into another nature because of the most perfect simplicity and immutability of the divine nature, divinity and humanity are not united in a unity of nature or of accident but in a unity of person and hypostasis. And because the divine nature cannot exist in any suppositum except in its own hypostasis, this union cannot exist in the hypostasis or person of man but rather of God. Hence by this union the first principle in one of its hypostases makes itself the suppositum of human nature, and thus there is only one personality and personal unity there, namely, on the part of the one assuming.

6. Lastly, because the Incarnation is from the first principle in so far as it repairs by conciliating, and in conciliating it is a mediator, and mediation properly falls to the Son of God, it follows that this is the case with the Incarnation. It is the mediator's part to be the medium between man and God, to lead man back to divine knowledge, conformity, and sonship. No one is more suitable as a medium than the person who produces and is produced, who is the middle one of the three persons. No one is more fitting to lead man back to the divine knowledge than the Word (by whom the Father expresses Himself), which is unitable to flesh, as a word is unitable to the voice. No one is more fitting to lead man back to divine conformity than He who is the image of the Father. No one is more fitting to lead man back to his adopted sonship than the natural Son. Hence no one is more fitting to become the Son of man than the Son of God.

7. Because the Son of man and of God is in every way the same by reason of the Incarnation and because "whatever things for one and the same reason are the same, are the same among themselves," [2] it follows that, unless there is a word

2 Aristotle, *I Elenchi*, chap. 5.

available for the purpose, one necessarily has to communicate by using an idiom, unless there is a word which includes a certain repugnance to one's idea, as is the case with those words used to express the union of one nature with another. Such words are: to unite, to be incarnate, to assume and be assumed. Such is the case with a denial of something whose opposite belongs to the other [nature], as is the case with the words: to begin to be, to be created, and the like in which an allied meaning exists contrary to the foregoing rule for the foregoing reason.

CHAPTER THREE

THE INCARNATION: ITS MODE

1. We must hold these truths about the mode of Incarnation: that the angel announced to the most Blessed Virgin Mary that the mystery of the Incarnation was to be accomplished in her, that the Virgin believed, was willing, and agreed, that the Holy Ghost descended upon her [3] to sanctify her and cause her conception. By His power "the Virgin conceived the Son of God whom the Virgin bore, and after His birth she remained a virgin." [4] She conceived not only the flesh but the flesh infused with a soul and united to the Word, liable to no sin but completely holy and immaculate. Hence she is called the Mother of God and the sweetest Virgin Mary.

2. The explanation of this is as follows: The Incarnation is a work that derives from the first principle, in so far as it is redemptive, in a most appropriate, all-embracing, and complete way. It befits His wisdom to work appropriately, His bounty to work in an all-embracing way, and His power to work perfectly.

3. Because the Incarnation derives from the first principle redeeming in a most appropriate way, and the appropriate

---

[3] Luke 1:26 ff.

[4] Augustine, *Sermo* 196 (alias 59), 1, 1; *Sermo* 51 (alias 63), 11, 18.

mode is that the medicine for the sickness should flow from contraries both as to the reparation for the fall and the remedy for the injury, for mankind had fallen by the suggestion of the devil, by the consent of a deceived woman, and by a generation motivated by a concupiscence communicating original sin to posterity, it was appropriate that on the contrary there should be the good angel leading to good, the Virgin believing and consenting to the proffered good, and the charity of the Holy Ghost sanctifying and fecundating for an immaculate conception so that thus "contraries might be cured by contraries" (Gregory, *Homilia in evangeliis*, II, 32, 1). Hence as a woman, deceived by the devil and known sensually and corrupted by man, transmitted sin, disease, and death to all mankind, so a woman, enlightened by the angel and sanctified and fecundated by the Holy Ghost, gave birth to an offspring, free from all the corruption of mind and body, who gives grace, health, and life to all who come to Him.

4. Because the Incarnation derives from the first principle redeeming in a most all-embracing way—for the fall of men and of angels is redeemed by the incarnate Word,[5] both those in heaven and on earth, and in the case of the fall of man, as regards both sexes—it was most proper, in order that the cure be all-embracing, that there should be a concourse of angel, woman, and man for the mystery of the Incarnation: the angel announcing, the virgin woman conceiving, and man the conceived offspring. Hence the angel Gabriel was the messenger of the eternal Father, the immaculate Virgin was the temple of the Holy Ghost, and the conceived offspring was the very person of the Word. Thus it was most fitting that in the all-embracing redemption there should be a concourse of the three in triple hierarchy, namely, the divine, the angelic, and the human, to represent not only the Trinity of God but also

[5] The redemption of man by the incarnation is considered by St. Thomas to be substantial; but in the case of the angels the redemption is only accidental since the angels are fixed in their decision and the redemption of the angels relates only to atonement. *De veritate*, q. 29.

the greatness of the benefit bestowed and the liberality of the supreme Redeemer. And because liberality is appropriate to the Holy Ghost, as is sanctification of the Virgin in whom the conception of the Word was accomplished, it follows that, though that work was done by the whole Trinity, yet by appropriation the Virgin is said to have conceived by the Holy Ghost.

5. Lastly, because the Incarnation comes from the first principle redeeming in a most complete way, it follows that in the conception there ought to be completeness in the offspring, the act of conception, and the conceiving power. Because the proper completeness ought to exist in the offspring, in the present conception there was not only an implanting of seed but a union, arrangement, and vivification by the soul and a deification by the united Deity so that the Virgin really conceived the Son of God because of a union of flesh with the Deity by the mediation of a rational spirit through whom the flesh was made suitable for union through a congruous medium.—Because there ought to be a proper completeness in the act of conception, and three of the four modes of producing man had already been used: the first from neither man nor woman, as in the case of Adam; the second from man without woman, as in the case of Eve; and the third from woman and man as in the case of all those who are born in concupiscence; it was fitting that for the completeness of all, the fourth way should be introduced, namely, from woman without the seed of man by the power of the supreme Operator.—Because there ought to be a proper completeness in power, it follows that in the conception of the Son of God there was a simultaneous concurrence of a power inborn, a power infused, and a power uncreated: the inborn power prepared the matter, the infused power separated it by purification, and the uncreated power perfected it instantly, a thing which could not have been done by a created power except successively. Thus the most holy Virgin Mary became a mother

in a most complete way by conceiving the Son of God Himself
without man through the fecundation of the Holy Ghost.
Because in the mind of the Virgin, the love of the Holy Ghost
alone glowed, the power of the Holy Ghost wrought wonderful things in her flesh, by a grace partly arousing, partly aiding, partly raising nature according to the exigency of that
wonderful conception.

CHAPTER FOUR

THE INCARNATION: THE FULLNESS OF TIME

1. We must hold these truths about the time of the Incarnation: that, though God could have been incarnate from the
beginning, He was unwilling to do so except at the end of
ages, after the law of nature and the law of prophecy had gone
before, after patriarchs and prophets to whom and through
whom the Incarnation was often promised. After these it was
proper for Him to become incarnate in the end of time and
the fullness thereof, as the Apostle says: "But when the fullness of time was come, God sent His Son made of a woman,
made under the law: that He might redeem them who were
under the law." [6]

2. The explanation of this is as follows: Because the Incarnation is the work of the first principle in reparation, it is
fitting that it happen in accord with the freedom of the will,
with the sublimity of the remedy, and with the integrity of
the universe, for the most wise Artificer saw to these in accomplishing all. Because freedom of the will requires that
the will be drawn into nothing unwillingly, it was thus fitting
that God should so redeem mankind that he who wished to
seek the Savior should find salvation, and he who was unwilling to seek the Savior should find no salvation. No one seeks

[6] Gal. 4:4.

a doctor unless he is aware of sickness, no one seeks a teacher unless he is aware he is ignorant, no one seeks aid unless he is aware of his impotence. Because man before his fall was well equipped with knowledge and power, God promised a time of the law of nature in which he should be conquered by ignorance. Afterwards man knew his ignorance but as to his power there remained a pride about which it is said that he who acts does not lack power, but he who orders lacks it. Then, God added a law, teaching with moral precepts and prescribing ceremonials so that when man came to knowledge and knew his impotency, man fled to divine mercy and sought grace which was given to us before the coming of Christ. Hence after the law of nature and of Scripture the incarnation of the Word ought to follow.

3. Again, because the sublimity of the remedy required that the Incarnation, a mystery most secret and most salutary, should be believed with most firm faith and should be loved with most ardent charity, it was most fitting that many testimonials of prophets should precede the coming of Christ, as explicit in words as it was implicit in figures, that what was secret should become certain and unquestionable for belief by many convincing testimonials. It was fitting that many promises and most ardent desires should precede the Incarnation so that the promised benefit should be expected, what was expected should be deferred, what was deferred should be sought more intensely, and what was long desired should be loved more fervently and be undertaken more fervently and accomplished more solicitously.

4. Lastly, because integrity and perfection of the universe require that all things should be ordered as to places and times, and the work of the Incarnation was the most perfect among all the divine works, and the procession ought to be from the imperfect to the perfect and not the converse, it follows that the Incarnation ought to occur at the end of time so that just as the first man, who was the sensitive ornament

of the whole world, was created last, namely, on the sixth day, for the completion of the whole world, so the second man, the complement of the whole world redeemed, in whom the first principle is joined with the last, namely, "God with clay," [7] should come into existence in the end of ages, and this is the sixth age which is the age proper for the exercise of wisdom, the suppression of concupiscence, and the transition from the state of unrest to rest. All these things belong to the sixth age of the world because of the incarnation of the Son of God.

5. Because the advent of Christ occurred in the time of the law of grace and in demonstration of the often promised mercy and in the beginning of the sixth age, and all these things bespeak a fullness of time since the law of grace fortifies the law of Scripture and the achievement of the promise perfects the promise, and the sixth age by reason of the sixfold perfection resounds in fullness, it follows that in the coming of the Son of God there is said to be a fullness of God, not because in His advent time was ended but because the mysteries of time were achieved. Just as Christ ought not to have come in the beginning of time, because His advent then would have been at a less opportune time, so He ought not to have deferred it to the end of time, because then it would be too late. It behooved the Savior to place the time of redemption between the time of sickness and the time of judgment. The mediator ought to precede certain of His members and to follow others. It behooved the perfect leader to show Himself at a time when there would be opportunity of running for the prize; and this is at the end of ages and before the termination of time and at the approach of the final judgment, so that, moved by fear of the judgment and attracted by the hope of reward and aroused by the perfection of an example, we must follow our leader enthusiastically and perfectly from virtue to virtue until we arrive at the reward of eternal bliss.[8]

---

[7] Bernard, *Sermo 3 in vigilia nativitatis Domini*, 8.
[8] Ps. 83:8.

CHAPTER FIVE

THE FULLNESS OF THE GRACE OF CHRIST AS REGARDS THE GIFTS IN OUR AFFECTIONS

1. After we have acquired a knowledge of the union of natures in the Word incarnate, we must consider the fullness of the spiritual gifts. In this connection, we must first consider the fullness of grace in the affections, then the fullness of wisdom in the intellect, and finally the fullness of merit in our works or the effect.

2. We must hold these truths as to the fullness of grace in the affections of Christ: that in Christ from His conception there was a fullness of all grace: the grace of a single person, of the head, and of the union. It was such that by the grace of the single person He had immunity from all fault both as to act and possibility because He neither sinned nor could sin. By the grace of the union He was worthy not only of the bliss of glory but also of latreuitic adoration, which is the worship of reverence due to God alone. By the grace of the head, He infuses motion and life in all who seek Him either through upright faith or by the sacraments of faith, in those who either preceded His advent or who follow it. "And they that went before and they that followed, cried, saying: 'Hosanna to the son of David.' " [9]

3. The explanation of this is as follows: Because reparation is an operation of the first principle such that it flows from Him with liberality and returns to Him in conformity, it is fitting that this should occur through grace and conformity to God. Grace flows from God freely and renders man godlike. Because the redeeming principle repairs through grace and everything exists more fully and perfectly in its own source and origin than elsewhere, it necessarily follows that in our

[9] Mark 11:9; Matt. 21:9.

redeeming principle, Christ the Lord, there was a fullness of all grace. And because the redeeming principle in reparation contains not only the cause of the principle, but the cause of the medium and of the end, of the end in satisfaction, of the medium in reconciliation and of the principle in an overflowing, it necessarily follows that in Christ there should have been a fullness of grace by reason of satisfaction by the end, reconciliation by the medium, and overflowing by the principle. Because, for the end to be suitable for satisfaction, it must be pleasing to God and hence perfectly free from all sin, and this could not be except by the gift of divine grace in some man, it was necessary to place in Christ grace sanctifying and confirming Him, and this we call the grace of the single person.

4. Again, because no medium is adapted to reconciliation except one who has in himself both natures, the higher and the lower, the adorable and the adoring, and this could never happen except by a most worthy union of grace, it was necessary to place in Christ grace above all grace and venerable by every kind of worship, and this we call the grace of union, through which Christ the man is over all things as God blessed and hence to be venerated by the worship of latria.

5. Lastly, because a principle is not effective in influence unless it has in itself the source and origin of fullness which is a fullness that is not only sufficient but superabundant, the Word incarnate was "full of grace and truth" [10] so that from His fullness all the just may be strengthened in the same way that all the members of the body receive motion and life from the head. Hence this grace is called the grace of the head because, as the head has in itself the fullness of the senses and is conformed to the other members and presides over them and bestows the benefit of its influence on the other members which are connected to the head itself, so Christ, having in Himself a superabundance of grace and being similar to us in nature, holy and just above all others, bestows on others

10 John 1:14.

who seek Him the benefit of grace and of the spirit through which spiritual beings possess sense and motion.

6. Because our quest of Him is stimulated by faith or the sacrament of faith, and the faith of Christ is the same in the past, present, and future, it follows that the reason for influence in Christ is posited for all, the past, the present, and the future, those believing in Christ and those reborn in Christ who are joined by faith to Christ and by the influence of grace become members of Christ and temples of the Holy Ghost [11] and hence sons of God the Father, united in turn by the indivisible chain of charity. Just as distance does not divide us, so we are not separated by intervals of time; hence all the just, wherever they are and whenever they are, constitute one mystical body of Christ by receiving sense and motion from the one influencing head which is the font, root, and origin of the fullness of all grace dwelling in Christ as in a font.

CHAPTER SIX

THE FULLNESS OF WISDOM IN HIS INTELLECT

1. We must hold this in regard to the fullness of wisdom in the intellect of Christ: that in the Word incarnate, namely, Christ our Lord, there was all fullness of wisdom as to things known, the modes of knowing, and the differences of knowledge. In Christ there was an eternal knowledge on the part of His divinity, a sense knowledge on the part of His sensual nature and flesh, and an abstract knowledge on the part of His mind and spirit, and thus there was a threefold knowledge: some knowledge through nature, some through grace, and some through glory. Hence He had wisdom both as God and as man, as the one comprehending all and as the wayfarer, as one enlightened by grace and as one uprightly formed

11 I Cor. 6:15, 19.

by nature. Thus in all there were in Christ five modes of knowledge. The first was according to divine nature, and in this way He knew all things actual and possible, finite and infinite, by an actual and complete knowledge. The second was through glory, and in this way he knew all things actual and finite by an actual and complete knowledge, but the infinite only by an extra knowledge due to that state. The third was through grace, and in this way He knew all things referring to the redemption of mankind. The fourth was according to the integral nature that Adam had, and in this way He knew all that referred to the constitution of the universe. The fifth was according to sense experience, and in this way He knew all that comes in contact with the sense organs, and of this mode it is said that "He learned obedience by the things which He suffered." [12]

2. The explanation of this is as follows: Just as it belongs to the redeeming principle to redeem us by a most generous grace, so too He redeems by a most provident wisdom. Because creation was according to the order of wisdom, redemption cannot be without light and the order of wisdom. Hence just as Christ ought to be free from all fault, so He ought to be removed from all ignorance and completely filled with the light and splendor of supernal wisdom. Hence He had a perfect knowledge in accord with each nature and cognitive power and in accord with all existing things.

3. Because things have existence in the eternal plan, in the human mind, and in their own genus, Christ necessarily had this threefold knowledge of things. Because a thing can be known in two ways in His plan, either by the Artificer Himself or by another viewing the plan, it similarly has to be and be known in His mind, except that He could not acquire this knowledge for that would be improper in Christ because it bespeaks imperfection; rather He possessed it as either an innate habit or an infused habit. Hence there were necessarily

12 Heb. 5:8.

to be found in Christ, as God and man, for the perfect fullness of knowledge, the five above-stated modes so that He knew things in the eternal plan, by the nature of His divinity and by the glory of understanding; in His own mind and by a natural or innate habit such as Adam and the angels knew; by a freely bestowed and infused habit as the saints of God enlightened by the Holy Ghost; in their own genus by the paths of sense, memory, and experience, which in us causes an unknown thing to be known, but in Christ it makes a thing that is known in one way to be known in another.

4. Because divine substance, power, and operation is immense, it follows that, according to the first mode of knowledge which is through the nature of divinity, He actually understands the infinite, for in some ineffable way, at the height of infinity, all infinity is finite.

5. Because the substance, power, and operation of the creature though it be of a higher level is finite so that the human mind does not rest except in the infinite good and it cannot comprehend that properly because the infinite is not comprehended by the finite if comprehension is properly understood, it follows that, as regards the second mode of knowing, the soul of Christ by the glory of comprehension achieved whatever knowledge it is possible for a finite nature, beatified by the infinite good to which it is united, to achieve. Hence it extended to things finite by actually comprehending them; to the infinite it did not extend except perchance in an infused way or by exceeding itself, for the soul cannot be equal to the Word in knowledge or in any other way.

6. Again, because grace looks mostly to the work of redemption, Christ, according to the third mode of knowledge, knew through a most perfect grace all that refers to our redemption much more acutely and better than any of the prophets or even the angels.

7. Further, because the nature of man, being well instituted, was created to be pre-eminent among all creatures and

to know what should be subservient to it as was clear in the creation of the first man, hence, according to the fourth mode of knowledge, Christ knew all that referred to the understanding of the earthly mechanism much more fully than did Adam.

8. Lastly, because a sense does not perceive things unless the object is present, Christ as regards His sensitive knowledge did not understand all things, but in one way some and in another way others as they offered an opportunity for achieving the redemption of mankind.

CHAPTER SEVEN

THE PERFECTION OF MERIT IN ITS EFFECT

1. We must hold these truths about the fullness of the merit of Christ: that in Christ our Lord all perfection and fullness of merit existed: first, as regards Him who achieved merit, who was not only man but also God. Second, as regards the time in which He achieved merit, because this ran from the instant of conception down to the very hour of death. Third, as regards that through which He achieved merit, because this was by the most perfect practice of charity and the most perfect exercise of virtue in praying, in doing, and in suffering. Fourth, as regards Him for whom He achieved merit, because He achieved merit not only for Himself but also for us, especially all the just. Fifth, as regards what He merited for us, because He merited not only glory but also grace and forgiveness, not only the glory of the spirit, but also the purification of the flesh and the opening of the celestial gates. Sixth, as regards what He merited for Himself, because, though He did not merit a glorification of the mind which He already had, yet He did merit the glorification of the body, the hastening of resurrection, the glorification of His name, and a dignity for

judicial power. Seventh, as regards the mode by which He achieved merit. Although one may be said to achieve merit in three ways, either by taking a new obligation, for what need not be done by doing what ought to be done, or for what to be done by doing more than ought to be done or for what ought to be done in one way by doing it in another, Christ achieved merit for us in all these ways, but only in the third way did He achieve merit for Himself, doing all by the fullness of the grace of the Holy Ghost and through this grace Christ was at the same time blessed and in the state for achieving merit so that all our merit must be founded on His merit.

2. The explanation of this is as follows: Because in the redeeming principle, that is, Christ our Lord, there necessarily was a fullness of grace and wisdom which are the source of our living upright and holy lives, there necessarily was in Christ a fullness and perfection of all merit, there being every mode of fullness. Because there was in Christ a fullness of the grace of union, and through this He was God from the instant of conception, having the glory of comprehension and the power of free will, there necessarily was a perfection of merit in Christ both as regards the supreme dignity of the one achieving merit and as regards preciseness of the opportuneness in the time element.

3. Again, because there was in Christ a fullness of the grace of the single person by which He had a most firm charity and all powers perfected in habit and exercise, it was necessary that there should be in Him a fullness of merit as regards the means by which He achieved merit, and to this belong the root of charity and the many acts of nobility.[13]

4. Further, because there was in Christ a fullness of the grace of the head by which He had the fullest influence over His members, He had fullness of merit as to Himself and as to us. Just as all spiritual things that we have flow from His divinity, so, by reason of the humanity He assumed, He mer-

---

13 Jerome, *Epistle* 148 (alias 14), 21.

ited for us those goods whether of our present state or of eternal joy.

5. Lastly, because the fullness of such gifts necessarily gave Christ the greatest and most perfect bliss in His higher nature though it was diluted in His state as wayfarer assumed because of us, He had the perfection of merit as regards what He merited for Himself because He not only had the glory and happiness enjoyed by the soul which quite naturally preceded all merit in Him, but He also possessed those things which the state of the wayfarer could not achieve, namely, purification of the flesh with the glorification of His own most excellent dignity.

6. Hence it is that Christ had the perfection of merit as regards the mode of achieving merit. Because He had a most perfect fullness from the instant of conception, He immediately merited all that He could merit with respect to Himself and hence what He ought to do in one way He could do in another, but for Himself He could not do what did not have to be done, or in the case of what He ought to do, He could not have done more, because He could not advance further in sanctity since He was most holy from the beginning. He did this for us who are justified through grace [14] by His merit that we may advance in justice and be crowned with eternal glory.

7. Hence in the merit of Christ are rooted all our merits whether they satisfy punishment or gain eternal life because we are unworthy to be absolved from offense against the highest good and are unworthy to gain the immensity of the eternal reward which is God, except by the merit of the God-man, to whom we can and should say: "Lord, Thou hast wrought all our works for us." [15] He is the Lord to whom the prophet said: "I have said to the Lord: Thou art my God, for Thou hast no need of my goods." [16]

[14] Rom. 3:24.
[15] Isa. 26:12.
[16] Ps. 15:2.

CHAPTER EIGHT

THE PASSION OF CHRIST: THE STATE OF THE SUFFERER

1. After considering the union of natures in the Word incarnate and the fullness of gifts, we ought to consider the endurance of sufferings. In this connection we ought to consider the state of the sufferer, the mode of suffering, and the results of the Passion.

2. We must hold these truths about the state of the sufferer: that Christ assumed not only human nature but also the defects associated with it. He assumed the bodily afflictions, namely, hunger, thirst, and fatigue. He assumed further the spiritual afflictions, namely, sadness, longing, and fear. But He did not assume all the bodily afflictions, such as many kinds of sickness, nor all the spiritual afflictions, such as ignorance and the rebelliousness of the flesh against the spirit. Nor did He assume the same kind of suffering as man, for He assumed suffering only in such a way that He could not suffer unwillingly but only according to the will of His divinity and according to the decision of His reason. And yet the suffering was in conflict with the desire of sensuality and the flesh, as this statement of our Savior shows: "Not as I will, but as Thou wilt." [17]

3. The explanation of this is as follows: Because the redeeming principle in reconciliation necessarily had the role of mediator, there necessarily was in Him a conflux of both extremes not only in natures but in those matters which are associated with a nature. Because God is just and happy, passionless, and immortal, and man in his fallen state is a sinner and miserable, passionate, and mortal, it was necessary that the mediator of God and man have justice and blessedness in

[17] Matt. 26:39.

common with God, passions and mortality in common with man, so that He could lead man back to God. Thus by having "a transient mortality and a permanent happiness," [18] He might lead man from his present misery back to the blessed life, just as the bad angel by possessing immortality with misery and injustice was the mediator leading man into sin and misery by his suggestion. Because Christ the mediator ought to have had innocence and the blessedness of productivity together with mortality and passion, He ought to have been at the same time a wayfarer and one comprehending all. He took something from every state for Himself, and hence it is said [19] He assumed from the state of innocence an immunity from sin, from the state of fallen nature mortality, from the true state of glory the blessedness of a perfect productivity.

4. Again, because the moral afflictions, namely, those four inflicted because of original sin (ignorance, infirmity, perversity, and concupiscence) cannot coexist with a most perfect innocence, Christ ought not to have assumed them, and He did not. Because those punishments which show the exercise of a perfect power and are testaments of true humanity and not of feigned humanity are the ones that look to His [human] nature in general, namely, hunger and thirst in the absence of food, sadness and fear in the presence of harm, it follows that He ought to have assumed these, and He did so.

5. Lastly, because no one who is innocent ought unwillingly to undertake any punishment, since this would be contrary to the order of divine justice, and because no mortal wishes to die or suffer, and this is in accord with the desire of nature which flees from death, it follows that Christ's afflictions ought to be of such a kind that He could suffer nothing without His consent. This is so not only because of the blessedness and omnipotent divinity united in Him by which He was able to repel all, but also because of His most perfect innocence which

[18] Augustine, *De civitate Dei*, IX, 15.
[19] Boethius, *De una persona et duabus naturis*, chap. 8.

in the order of natural justice is not allowed to suffer anything unwillingly. And He ought to have had such afflictions that His suffering was contrary to the inclination and desire of [man's] nature which is for sensuality and the flesh. Hence Christ followed reason in His prayer and repressed the desire of the flesh and by this fled from passion, for He said: "Let this chalice pass from Me." [20] He conformed the will of reason to the will of the Father and preferred it to the desire of the flesh when He said: "But yet not My will, but Thine be done." [21] Thus one will was not contrary to the other because "according to the divine will He wished what was just, according to the will of reason He agreed with justice, but according to the will of the flesh He declined punishment but did not affront justice. Hence each will achieved what was its own and followed what pertained to each, the divine will justice, the rational will obedience, the will of the flesh nature." [22] Hence there was in Christ no struggle or resistance, but a peaceful arrangement and ordered tranquillity.

CHAPTER NINE

THE PASSION OF CHRIST: THE MODE OF SUFFERING

1. We must hold these truths about the mode of suffering: that Christ suffered a most general passion, a most severe passion, a most ignominious passion, and a destructive yet life-giving passion. He suffered a most general passion as regards His human nature, not only in all the main members of His body but also in all the powers of His soul though He could suffer nothing as regards His divine nature. He suffered a

[20] Matt. 26:39.
[21] Luke 22:42.
[22] Hugh of St. Victor, *Libello de quattuor voluntatibus in Christo.*

most severe passion by bearing not only the pain of one suffering from wounds, but by bearing the extra pain of one
suffering for our crimes. He suffered a most ignominious passion because of the yoke of the cross which was one of the
worst punishments, and because of association with the wicked,
namely, thieves, He "was with the wicked." [23] He suffered a
most destructive passion by the separation of soul from body,
yet the union of both with His divinity was preserved. He is
anathema who says the Son of God at any time relinquished
the nature which He had once assumed.

2. The explanation of this is as follows: Since the redeeming principle ought to have redeemed man ordinately just as
it had produced him ordinately, it ought so to redeem him
that his freedom of will would be preserved and nonetheless
the honor of God and the order governing the universe be
preserved. Because He ought to redeem man and yet preserve
freedom of the will, He redeemed man by giving a most efficacious example. That example is most efficacious which invites and instructs one to the height of virtue. Nothing, however, better instructs man in virtue than the example of one
enduring death on account of divine justice and obedience,
not ordinary death but death entirely as a punishment. Nothing incites man to achievement more than such benignity as
caused the great Son of God to lay down His life [24] for us who
are without merit but with many faults. This benignity showed
itself the greater by the fact that He undertook very severe
and abject sufferings for us and wished so to suffer. God, who
"spared not even His own Son; but delivered Him up for us
all, how hath He not also, with Him, given us all things?" [25]
By this we are invited to love Him and, having loved Him, to
imitate Him.

3. Again, because He ought to have redeemed man and yet

23 Isa. 53:12. Cf. Mark 15:28: Luke 22:37.
24 I John 3:16.
25 Rom. 8:32.

to have preserved the honor of God, He redeemed him by offering a series of satisfactions. "Satisfying the honor of God is rendering what is due to Him." [26] Pride and disobedience with regard to what man is bound to do detracted from the honor of God. Hence there was no better method of restoration than by humiliation and obedience in a matter where He was not bound. Because Jesus Christ in so far as He was God was equal to the Father in the form of God and in so far as He was man was not innocent and was the debtor of death, He, in emptying Himself and "becoming obedient unto death," [27] "paid God that which He took not away" [28] by achieving perfect satisfaction and proferred a sacrifice of the greatest sweetness for the perfect placation of God.

4. Lastly, because He ought to have redeemed man to preserve the order governing the universe, He redeemed man by a most suitable medium. It is most fitting that contraries should be cured by contraries. Because man, wishing to be as wise as God, sinned by desiring to taste of the forbidden tree and hence is inclined to pleasure and hardened in presumption, and because the whole of mankind was thereby infected, lost immortality, and incurred a deserved death, hence that man might be redeemed by a fitting medium, God was made man and wished to be humiliated and to suffer on the tree and, in contrast to the universal infection, to suffer a most general passion; in contrast to pleasure, to suffer a most severe passion; in contrast to presumption, to suffer a most ignominious passion; in contrast to a deserved and unwilling death, to suffer an undeserved death voluntarily.

5. Because the general nature of corruption in us had infected not only our body and soul but even every power of our soul, Christ suffered in every part of His body and in every power of His soul. He suffered in the higher part of the reason,

---

[26] Anselm, *Cur Deus homo*, chaps. 11 and 20.
[27] Phil. 2:6–8.
[28] Ps. 68:5.

which seeks its chief delight in God as reason, because of His union to the highest nature, and He suffered extremely in His nature because of His union to the lower nature, for Christ was at the same time a wayfarer and one comprehending all.

6. Again, because pleasure so strongly infects our soul and flesh as is shown by the carnal and spiritual sins, Christ suffered a most severe passion in His flesh and a most bitter passion in His soul. And because in His flesh there was perfection of physical constitution and complete vigor of senses and in His soul there was the greatest love for God and our neighbor, the pain due to both was most intense.

7. Further, because the tumor of pride sometimes develops internally from presumption and sometimes externally from ostentation and other praise, Christ suffered both types of ignominy for the remedy of all pride, both by Himself and with the companions He had in His passion.

8. Finally, because all these matters did not pertain to His divine and passionless nature but only to His human nature, there was a division of soul from flesh in the death of Christ such that the unity of person was still preserved and likewise the union of the flesh and of the soul with His divinity. And because the union of the soul with the body makes one a man and makes him live, Christ was not a man in that triduum though the soul and flesh were united with the Word. Whence, because death in human nature could not induce death in the person which lives forever, death died in His life and by the death of Christ "death is swallowed up in victory"; [29] the chieftain of death is vanquished, and hence man is freed from death and the cause of death by the merit of the death of Christ, through a most efficacious medium.

[29] I Cor. 15:54.

CHAPTER TEN

THE PASSION OF CHRIST: THE TERMINATION OF THE PASSION

1. We must unquestionably hold these truths about the termination of the passion of Christ and its fruits: that the soul of Christ after the Passion descended into the depths, to limbo, to release not all, but only those among the members of Christ who had persevered by a living faith or by the sacraments of faith. After this, on the third day, He arose from the dead and resumed the body which He had previously inhabited but not in such a state as it had previously been. Before this His body had been passible and mortal, but after He arose, it was impassible and immortal, living forever. Finally, after forty days He ascended into heaven where He is exalted above every creature and sits at the right hand of the Father.[30] What has been said is to be understood not as regards place, which is not fitting to God the Father, but as regards the excellence of the good, for He resides in the more potent goods of the Father. Finally, after an interval of ten days, He sent the Holy Ghost upon the apostles as He had promised, for through Him the Church of the nations is gathered and directed in accord with the various distributions made of graces and duties.

2. The explanation of this is as follows: Just as Christ, in so far as He is the uncreated Word, formed all things most perfectly; so, in so far as He was incarnate, He ought to reform all things most perfectly. It is fitting that the most perfect principle should not effect a work less than perfect, and therefore the redeeming principle ought to have achieved human redemption to perfection. To the end that His work be most perfect, it ought to be most sufficient and most efficacious.

3. Because His redemption is most sufficient, it extended to

[30] Mark 16:19; Acts 1:1 ff.

things celestial, terrestrial, and infernal. Because through Christ things infernal are released, things terrestrial are redeemed, and things celestial are reintegrated, the first being accomplished by pardon, the second by grace, and the third by glory; hence, after the Passion His soul descended into hell [limbo] to release those detained there: then He arose from the dead to raise to life those dead in sins; then He ascended into heaven to lead captivity back [31] to the reintegration of the heavenly Jerusalem and sent the Holy Ghost to reconstruct the earthly Jerusalem. All these things follow necessarily and are required for the completeness of human redemption.

4. Again, because His redemption was most efficacious alike in those who follow Him and have acceded or are acceding to Christ, in those who were His members, and in those who are, and such belong to Him through faith, hope, and charity, it follows that that remedy ought to have had its efficacy first in those who believed in Christ and by believing hoped and by hoping loved Him. He ought therefore to have immediately descended to those in hell [limbo] to release them. Hence the gates of heaven were opened by the passion of Christ, who by His satisfaction had removed the sword and by changing the divine sentence had snatched all His members from hell [limbo].

5. He ought to have had an extraordinary influence on those who follow the advent of Christ so that He may lead them to heavenly glory by advancing in faith, hope, and charity. That He might lay the basis for the faith by which we believe Christ is true man and true God and by which we believe that He willed to redeem us by His death and to be able to lead us to life by His resurrection, He willed to arise to an immortal life after a fitting interval of time had elapsed, namely, thirty-six hours, which would show that He was truly dead. He ought not to have been more hasty lest, if He had arisen earlier, it might be believed that He had not been truly dead but had

[31] Ps. 67:19.

feigned death. He ought not to have deferred it longer lest He should lie forever in death and it might be believed that He was powerless and that He was unable to recall anyone to life. Thus it is that He arose on the third day.[32]

6. Further, that He might raise hope, He ascended to the heavenly glory which we hope for. But because hope does not arise except from a faith in future immortality, He did not ascend immediately but only after an interval of forty days during which He demonstrated by many signs and arguments the truth of the Resurrection by which the soul is strengthened in faith and raised to the level of hoping for the heavenly glory.

7. Finally, that He might inflame our love, He sent the fire of the Holy Ghost on Pentecost. Because no one is filled with this fire unless he wishes it, seeks it, and throbs with a present and thirsting desire for it founded on hope, He did not send the Holy Ghost immediately after the Ascension but only after an interval of ten days during which the disciples were disposing themselves for the reception of the Holy Ghost by gathering together, praying, and longing for Him. Hence, just as He spent a fitting interval in suffering, so the interval was proper in arising from the dead, in ascending to heaven, and in sending the Holy Ghost both because of the basis for the three powers mentioned above and because of the many mysteries which are implied in these statements of time.

8. And because the Holy Ghost, who is love and is achieved by love, is the source of all gifts, when He descended, He poured out a fullness of gifts to achieve the mystical body of Christ, and because there ought to be different members in a perfect body, different duties and exercises for the different members, and different gifts for different duties, it follows that the Spirit gives to one the word of wisdom, to another the word of knowledge, to another faith, to another the grace of healing, "to another the working of miracles, to another proph-

[32] I Cor. 15:4.

ecy, to another the discerning of spirits, to another diverse
kinds of tongues, and to another interpretation of speeches,
but all these things one and the same Spirit worketh, dividing to every one according as He will." [33] And this is all according to His most generous providence and most provident
bounty.

[33] *Ibid.,* 12:8–11.

PART FIVE

THE GRACE OF THE HOLY GHOST

CHAPTER ONE

GRACE: A GIFT DIVINELY GIVEN

1. After the treatise on the incarnation of the Word, which is the source and fountain of every gratuitous gift, something must be said about the grace of the Holy Ghost. We can consider the grace of the Holy Ghost from four different angles: first, in so far as it is a gift divinely given; second, in its relation to free choice; third, in its relation to the series of virtues; fourth, in its relation to the apportioning of rewards.

2. As to grace, as a gift divinely given, we must hold that it is in itself a gift because it is given by God and flows immediately from Him. The Holy Ghost is given with it and in it for He is an uncreated, excellent, and perfect gift "coming down from the Father of lights" through the incarnate Word. According to John in the Apocalypse, he saw a stream, "clear as crystal, proceeding from the throne of God and of the Lamb." [1] Nevertheless, grace is a gift by which the soul is perfected and becomes the bride of Christ, the daughter of the eternal Father, and the temple of the Holy Ghost. This could not be brought about except through the dignifying condescension and condescending dignity of His eternal majesty through the gift of His own grace. Grace, therefore, is a gift which cleanses, enlightens and perfects the soul, brings it to life, reforms it and strengthens it, lifts it up, likens and joins it to God and thereby makes it acceptable to God. Hence a gift of this kind is rightfully called and ought to be named a *gratia gratum faciens*.[2]

---

[1] Jas. 1:17; Apoc. 22:1.

[2] By *gratia gratum faciens* Catholic theologians mean the grace that makes the soul of its recipient holy and pleasing to God. Such is sanctifying grace.

All graces are the gratuitous gift of God. But some of them are bestowed

3. The explanation of this is as follows: Since the first principle productive for its own supreme benevolence made a rational soul capable of eternal happiness, and since the reparative principle restored to health that capacity after it had been rendered ineffective through sin, and since eternal happiness consists in the possession of the highest good and this is God, a good far excelling all the dignity of human worship, it follows that no one is worthy of attaining that highest good, since it is entirely above all the limitations of nature, unless man is lifted above himself by the condescension of God. God, however, does not condescend through His own immutable essence but through an influence flowing from Him. Our spirit is not elevated above itself through a change of location but through a godlike series. Therefore, the rational soul in order to be worthy of eternal happiness must necessarily become a partaker of godlike influence. This godlike influence because it is from God, according to God and because of God restores the image of our mind to conformity with the Blessed Trinity, not only in the order of origin but also in the correctness of choice and the calm of achievement. Because he who possesses those qualities is led directly back to God, just as he is immediately conformed to Him, that gift is given directly by God, the inflowing principle, so that as the image of God emanates directly from God, so there emanates immediately from Him the similitude of God which is the godlike perfection of the divine image and is therefore called the image of the restoration.

4. Again, because he who enjoys God possesses God, it fol-

---

primarily for the sake of persons other than the recipient. They are called *gratiae gratis datae.* Such are the extraordinary charismata and the ordinary powers of the priesthood. The possession of these graces does not exclude personal unholiness. For St. Bonaventure's use of the expression *gratiae gratis datae,* see *infra,* especially pp. 145 f.

Meritum de condigno is merit in a strict sense, supposing an equality between service and reward. Its claim to reward is on the basis of strict justice.

Meritum de congruo receives a reward, not on the ground of strict justice, but only of equity; it depends on the liberality of the giver.

lows that when grace, which by its own likeness to God disposes one for the enjoyment of God, is given, the uncreated gift which is the Holy Ghost accompanies it, and he who possesses this gift possesses God as well.

5. And because no one possesses God unless He is possessed by Him and because no one possesses and is possessed by Him unless he particularly and incomparably loves Him and is loved by Him just as the bride is loved by the bridegroom and because no one is so loved unless he is adopted for eternal inheritance as a son, hence *gratia gratum faciens* makes the soul the temple of God, the spouse of Christ, and a child of the eternal Father. And because this is impossible without God's consent and condescension, it cannot happen through some infusion which is acquired naturally but must come through a gift divinely and freely infused. This is especially evident if one considers how great it is to be the temple of God, the son of God, indissolubly and, as it were, matrimonially united to God by the bond of love and grace.

6. Lastly, because our mind is not made to conform to the Blessed Trinity in correctness of choice except through the vigor of virtue, the splendor of truth, and the fervor of love, and the vigor of virtue cleanses, steadies, and elevates the spirit, the splendor of truth enlightens the soul, reshapes it, and likens it to God, the fervor of love perfects the soul, revives it, and joins it to God, and because through all these man stands pleasing and acceptable to God, it follows that this godlike influence is said to have all ten of the above-mentioned qualities so that it is encompassed by the last-mentioned as a most complete enumeration. It is called *gratia gratum faciens* because it makes him who possesses it pleasing to God since it is not only given freely by God but is also according to God and on account of God because it exists so that through grace the work flowing from God is turned back in the manner of a rational circle to God in whom is contained the complement of all rational spirits.

CHAPTER TWO

GRACE: AN AID TO MERITORIOUS GOOD

1. In the second place, the grace of the Holy Ghost comes up for our consideration in relation to free choice in two respects: first, in so far as it is an aid to merit; second, in so far as it is a remedy for sin.

2. As to the grace of God as an aid for merit, the following must be held: Though grace is called general, special, and proper, it is called general to denote it as a divine aid freely and liberally imparted to a creature and as indifferent in regard to any act. Without this kind of aiding grace we are unable to do anything or to continue in existence. Grace is called special when it is divinely given as an aid so that he who has prepared himself for the reception of the gift of the Holy Ghost may attain the state of merit with it, and such is called *gratia gratis data,* and without it no one can adequately do what it is in his power to do, namely, prepare himself for salvation. Grace is called proper when the aid is divinely given to render someone worthy, and this is called the gift of *gratia gratum faciens,* without which no one can render himself worthy or accomplish good or reach eternal salvation. As the root of merit, grace precedes all merit. Because of this it is said that "it precedes the will in order that it may will, it follows close after, however, lest the will act in vain." [3] Hence no one can merit grace *de condigno,* but grace "merits to be increased by God for us in this life so that, having been increased, it also merits to be perfected" [4] in the fatherland [heaven] and in everlasting glory by God Himself, to whom it belongs to infuse, increase, and perfect grace according to the coopera-

[3] Augustine, *Enchiridion,* XXXII, 9.
[4] Augustine, *Epistle* 186 (alias 106), III, 10.

tion of our will and in accordance with the purpose and good pleasure of eternal predestination.

3. The explanation of this is as follows: Since the first principle by His omnipotent power and most blessed liberality brought every creature from nothingness to being, and thus a creature of itself has non-being, and its whole being comes from elsewhere, it follows that the creature was so made that it would always stand in need of the first principle because of its own deficiency, and the first principle because of His own benevolence does not cease to sustain it. Because the rational spirit is in itself defective in that it is from nothing and by its limited and needy nature is turned back upon itself in loving its own good and by the fact that its whole being is from God, it is totally subject to God, and because the rational spirit in its defectiveness tends of itself to non-being, and because being turned back on itself does not through itself rise to the righteousness of perfect justice, and because being is totally subject to God and, since God has no need for its good, it cannot, except through the divine condescension, do anything by itself and its own power, and for this reason only by divine condescension does the rational spirit make God debtor to it especially as regards the eternal reward which is God, it follows that for the rational being to be saved in its very being, since it is defective, it is always dependent on the aid of the divine presence, conservation, and influence through which it is preserved in being. And this although it is universal in all creatures is still called by the name of grace because it proceeds not from something owing to us but from the bounty of divine goodness. Hence it also follows that, in order for one to prepare himself for the gift of heavenly grace, since he is turned back toward himself, he needs the gift of another *gratia gratis data,* especially after the fall of nature. Through this grace man is made capable of moral goods, which are good only by reason of circumstances, which cannot be called good unless they derive from the right intention, namely, not be-

cause of us but because of the highest good to which our spirit which tends to curve back on ourselves does not rise unless it is preceded by God with some *gratia gratis data*. Hence that man may make his works deserving of eternal reward, since he is entirely dependent on God and entirely His debtor, he needs the gift of *gratia gratum faciens* through which God condescends to him, God accepting His own image and will rather than an act flowing from this image. Since "the cause is nobler than the effect," [5] no one is able to improve himself or to make his work pleasing to God unless he himself first is pleasing to God, who considers the person himself before his works. Therefore the root of all merit lies in the *gratia gratum faciens*, which has the power to make man worthy of God. Hence no one is able to gain that grace *de condigno* but only *de congruo*.

4. When we possess this grace, through its good use an increase of it is merited *de digno* in our state of wayfarers. Since God alone is the principle and source of the flow of this grace, He alone is the principle of its increase by way of infusion, and grace by way of merit and worthiness, and free will by way of cooperating and meriting, in so far as the free will cooperates with grace and makes its own what belongs to grace.

5. Therefore free will through grace not only merits *de digno* an increase of grace for us in this life, but likewise merits *de condigno* its fullness for us in the fatherland [heaven]. This will occur because of the sublimity of the Holy Ghost's gift cooperating in gaining merit, because of the veracity of God who promises, because of the ability to choose possessed by the free will of the one who consents and finally perseveres in his choice, because of the difficulty involved in gaining merit, because of the dignity of Christ our mediator and head, since He ought to be glorified with His members, because of the liberality of God who rewards, for it is not fitting that He should give little in return for homage faithfully accorded Him, and

[5] Avicenna, *Metaphysics*, tr. 6, 3.

because of the nobility of a work springing from love, which has only as much weight in the eyes of the judge as the love from which it springs, for this love prefers God to all creatures and hence cannot be rewarded sufficiently and fully except in God and the highest good. For all these seven reasons a seven-fold grace makes it possible for man to merit eternal glory not only *de congruo* but also *de condigno*.

CHAPTER THREE

GRACE: A REMEDY FOR SIN

1. As to grace in so far as it is a remedy for sin, this must be held: that although free will is "under God most powerful," [6] yet by itself it can fall into sin, but cannot rise without the aid of that divine grace which is called *gratum faciens*. That grace, although it is sufficient as a remedy for sin, is not infused in an adult unless there is present the consent of his free will. Hence for the justification of an impious man four things are needed, namely, the infusion of grace, the expulsion of guilt, con-trition, and movement of free will. Sin is expelled by the gift of God, not by free will, but not without free will. It belongs to *gratia gratis data* to recall free will from evil and to arouse it to good, and it is the function of free will to consent or to dissent. It belongs to one so consenting to receive grace, and to one receiving grace to cooperate with it so that he may attain salvation.

2. The explanation of this is as follows: Since the first prin-ciple by the very fact that it is first and most powerful is the cause of all things which are in the universe except sins, "which are transgressions of the divine law and infringements on the heavenly decrees," [7] nothing is rebellious, hateful, and offen-

6 Bernard, *De gratia et libero arbitrio*, III, 7; IV, 9.
7 Ambrose, *Liber de paradiso*, VIII, 39.

sive to Him except sin, which by despising the law of God
and by turning us away from the immutable good offends God,
mars the free will, destroys the gratuitous gift and binds one
to eternal punishment. Since the deformation of the image
and the destroying of grace is, as it were, the annihilation of
the existence of moral life and the life of grace, and since an offense against God must be measured with reference to God
Himself, and since the guilt deserving eternal punishment
must be looked upon as infinite, it is impossible that man rise
from sin unless he be restored to the life of grace, the offense
remitted, and the eternal punishment abated. He alone who
is the creative principle is also the re-creative principle,
namely, the eternal Word of the Father who is Jesus Christ,
the mediator of God and men, who because He creates all
things from nothing, creates them by Himself alone without
any intermediary.

3. Because He re-creates by reforming through the habit of
grace and justice what was deformed through the vice of sin,
and re-creates by removing through condign satisfaction what
was subject to punishment, it follows that He redeems us by
bearing the punishment for us in an assumed nature and by
infusing reformative grace which, because it unites us with
its origin, makes us members of Christ. Thus He makes the
sin-infested soul which had been an enemy of God, harlot of
the devil, and servant of sin, the spouse of Christ, the temple
of the Holy Ghost, and the child of the eternal Father. All this
happens through the gratuitous and condescending infusion
of a gratuitous gift.

4. Again, because God restores us in such a manner that
He does not nullify the established natural laws, He gives
this grace to free will in such a way that grace does not force
it but its consent remains free. Hence also for the expulsion
of sin, it is not only necessary that grace be introduced but
also that there be the concurrence of free will by adults, by
adults I say, because the faith of the Church and the merit

of Christ suffice in the case of children and excuse their impotence. It is necessary that man adapt himself for the expulsion of guilt through the abhorrence of all sins, and we call this contrition. It is also necessary that man adapt himself for the introduction of grace through the entertainment and acceptance of the divine gift, and we call this the act of the free will. These four things are necessary for the justification of an impious man.

5. Lastly, because the predisposition to a completive form ought to be in conformity with it; and for free will to dispose itself for *gratia gratum faciens,* it needs the assistance of *gratia gratis data;* and because it is not the part of grace to force the free will but to anticipate it, and it is the part of both at the same time to proceed to the act, it follows that the act of the free will and of grace concur in our justification in a consonant and orderly way so that it belongs to *gratia gratis data* to stir the free will, but it is for the free will to consent to this stimulation or to reject it. And it is for the consenting will to prepare itself for the *gratia gratum faciens* because in so doing the will does what in it lies; and *gratia gratum faciens* has to be infused in one thus disposed, whose free will can cooperate, if it wishes, and thus merit; or it can oppose the grace through sin and then incur demerit. If the will cooperates with grace to the very end, it merits the attainment of eternal salvation.

6. It is true as Augustine says: "He who has created you without you, will not justify you without yourself." [8] It is also true that, "It is not of him that willeth, nor of him that runneth, but of God that showeth mercy." [9] And likewise, no one can be proud concerning his merits because God crowns nothing in us except His own gifts. God has reserved for Himself the liberal bestowing of the gifts of grace so that man may learn not to be ungrateful, not to glory in himself as if he were not beholden, but may learn to glory in the Lord. Although

---

[8] Augustine, *Sermo* 169 (alias 15), XI, 13.
[9] Rom. 9:16.

free will cannot of itself fulfill the law or gain grace, yet it is inexcusable if it does not do what it can, because *gratia gratis data* is always ready at hand, and by its aid man can do what it is in him to do. When this is done, man may possess *gratia gratum faciens,* and when this has been obtained, man may fulfill the divine law and do the will of God. When this in turn has been done, man may attain eternal beatitude because of meritorious works which come entirely from grace and also entirely from free will though principally from grace, because as Augustine says, "grace is to be compared to free will as the rider to the horse." [10] The rider directs the free will, leads and persuades it to the portal of eternal happiness by exercising us in works of perfect virtue according to the gift of the sevenfold grace.

CHAPTER FOUR

THE DIVISION OF GRACE INTO THE HABITS OF THE VIRTUES

1. In the third place, we must consider grace in relation to the habits of virtues, and this involves three matters: the first is how one grace branches out into habits of virtues; the second is how it branches out into the habits of the gifts; the third is how it branches out into habits of beatitudes.

2. As to the branching out of grace into habits of virtues, this must be held: that, though there is one grace refreshing the soul, there are nevertheless seven gratuitous virtues by which human life is governed: three are theological, namely, faith, hope, and charity, and four are cardinal, namely, prudence, temperance, fortitude, and justice, which in one way is a common and general virtue, and in another way special and proper. These seven virtues, though they are distinct and

10 Augustine, *Hypognosticon,* III, 11.

have their own excellences, are mutually coherent and equal to one another in the same person; and though they are gratuitous, having been formed through grace, yet, with the exception of charity, they can be deformed through sin, and can be reformed through repentance with the aid of grace which is the origin, the end, and the form of the habits of virtues.

3. The explanation of this is as follows: As the productive principle in His own height of perfection in giving the life of nature gives life not only as to the first act, but as to the second act, which is operation; so the restoring principle necessarily must bestow life gratuitously on the spirit as to its being, both as regards being and as regards operation. Because, in one living in accordance with the one prime life there are many vital operations for the perfect manifestation of that life, since an act is made diverse through its objects, and diversity of acts requires distinction of habits,[11] it follows that, though the vivifying grace is one, yet it necessarily has to be divided into various habits because of the various operations. Because some moral deeds are primary, like believing, and some are intermediate, like understanding what is believed, and some are truly last, like seeing what is understood, and because in the first the soul is rectified, in the second it is advanced, and in the third it is perfected, hence *gratia gratum faciens* is divided into habits of virtues whose function it is to rectify the soul, into habits of the gifts whose function is to advance the soul, and into habits of the beatitudes whose function it is to perfect the soul.

4. Again, because a perfect rectification of the soul requires that it be rectified in two respects, namely, upper and lower, both with regard to the end and with regard to those things that tend to the end, consequently the soul must be rectified in regard to its upper aspect, in which the image of the eternal Trinity rests, through the three theological virtues, so that, just as the image of creation consists in a trinity of powers

11 Aristotle, *De anima*, chaps. 4 ff.

with a unity of essence, so the image of re-creation consists in a trinity of habits with a unity of grace, through which the soul is borne directly to the highest Trinity according to the three appropriations of the three persons. Thus faith directs one in believing and assenting to what is supremely true, hope in initiating and expecting what is supremely arduous, charity in desiring and loving what is supremely good.

5. The soul must be rectified in its lower aspect through the four cardinal virtues. Prudence rectifies the rational, fortitude the irascible, temperance the concupiscible, but justice rectifies all these powers in one's relation to another. Since this "other" can be a definite neighbor, and it is even possible for the same man to be related to himself as to another, as God Himself can be so related; hence justice is said to embrace all powers.[12] It is called not only a cardinal virtue but also a general virtue, comprising the rectitude of the whole soul since it is referred to as the "rectitude of the will." [13] Hence it comprises not only the virtues relating to one's neighbor such as equity and liberality, but those relating to one's self such as penance and innocence, and those relating to God such as adoration, piety, and obedience.

6. Finally, because all the rectitude of the virtues according to its gratuitous being flows from grace as its origin and root, and according to its meritorious being is related to charity as its origin, form, and end, hence the other gratuitous virtues as habits are interrelated, and as meritous acts are equal. Thus it is that the other habits of virtues can be deformed, with the exception of charity alone which is the form of the virtues. When we possess virtues without grace and charity which constitute their life, they are deformed. When abundant grace is infused, the virtues assume a form and ornamentation and become acceptable to God just as colors with-

---

12 Augustine, *De generatione contra Manichaeos,* X, 14.
13 Anselm, *De conceptu virginis et originalis peccati,* chap. 3; *Dialogus de veritate,* chap. 12.

out light are invisible but in the presence of light become clear, beautiful, and pleasing to the eye. Just as from light and color comes unity of the stimulus, and one light suffices for the illumination of many colors, similarly out of grace and unformed habits when they are reformed comes a unity in the sense of being meritorious and gratuitous; yet one grace suffices for the forming and infusion with grace of various habits.

CHAPTER FIVE

THE DIVISION OF GRACE INTO HABITS OF THE GIFTS

1. As to the division of grace into habits of the gifts, we must hold these truths: although many are the gifts of *gratia gratis data,* and generally all habits divinely given can rightly be called gifts of God, yet in a special and appropriate sense there are seven gifts of the Holy Ghost which Isaias enumerates and names, when he speaks about the flower which sprang from the root of Jesse, that is, Christ. For of Him Isaias says, that the "Spirit of the Lord shall rest upon Him: the spirit of wisdom and of understanding, the spirit of counsel and of fortitude, the spirit of knowledge and of godliness. And He shall be filled with the spirit of fear of the Lord." [14] He proceeds in a descending enumeration from the highest and so combines that he shows at the same time the distinction, connection, origin, and order of the gifts.

2. The explanation of this is as follows: Since the restoring principle through His great liberality gives grace not only for making straight the crooked path of our vices through the habits of the virtues but also for removing the hindrances of the consequences of vice through the habits of the gifts, it fol-

[14] Isa. 11:2 f.

lows that the gratuitous gifts must be increased in proportion to what is necessary for sufficient advance. Because our soul needs to advance in seven ways, the gifts of the Holy Ghost must be sevenfold because of the sevenfold cause. The soul depends on them for advance against the crookedness of the vices, as much for the natural powers as for the superadded virtues, in suffering, in doing, in contemplating, and their combination.

3. First, because the unfortunate results of the vices must be repelled, there are seven gifts of the Holy Ghost, namely, fear against pride, piety against envy, knowledge against anger, which is a kind of insanity,[15] fortitude against sloth which renders the mind weak as regards the good, counsel against covetousness, understanding against gluttony, and wisdom against lust.

4. Second, for the advancement of the natural powers there ought to be seven gifts of the Holy Ghost. The irascible needs to be advanced to the good as much in good fortune as in adversity: in good fortune it is advanced by fear, in adversity by fortitude. The concupiscible needs to be advanced to love of the neighbor, which comes through piety, and to love of God, which comes through a taste for wisdom. The rational depends for its advancement on contemplation of, choice of, and pursuit of truth. Through the gift of understanding the rational is directed to the contemplation of truth, through the gift of counsel in the choosing of truth, through the gift of knowledge to the pursuit of what is chosen, for through the gift of knowledge we are directed to the right "in the midst of a crooked and perverse generation." [16]

5. Third, in order that the functions of the seven virtues may prosper there must be seven gifts of the Holy Ghost. Fear advances one to temperance and restrains the flesh, piety leads to true justice, knowledge to prudence, fortitude to bravery

---

[15] Cicero, *Disputationes Tusculanes*, IV, 23.
[16] Phil. 2:15.

or patience, counsel to hope, understanding to faith, and wisdom to charity. As "love is the mother and end of all virtues," [17] so wisdom is of gifts, for the Book of Wisdom rightly says: "All good things came to me together with her, and innumerable riches through her hands." [18]

6. Fourth, seven are the habits of the gifts designed for our ability to suffer like Christ. However, in the case of Christ, the will of His Father, human necessity, and the strength of virtue moved Him to endure. The divine will moved Him since it was made known through understanding, loved through wisdom, and held in reverence through fear. Our necessity moved Christ, and knowledge is necessary to understand this, and piety is superadded to have pity on our need. The strength of virtue moved Christ, since He was made farsighted in His choice through counsel and strong in achievement through fortitude. Thus there ought to be seven gifts.

7. Fifth, there are seven gifts of the Holy Ghost designed for our acting. For unimpeded accomplishment we must be aided in turning away from evil, and this comes through fear. We must also be aided in our quest of the twofold good: either the good of necessity or of supererogation. As to the first, we are aided through knowledge and piety so that the one guides and the other executes. As to the second, we are aided through counsel which guides and fortitude which executes. We necessarily must repose in the best, and this will be in proportion to our understanding of truth and our love of good. The first comes through the gift of understanding, the second through the gift of wisdom in which there is rest.

8. Sixth, for advancement in contemplation the gifts of the Holy Ghost are seven in number. The soul must be cleansed, illuminated, and perfected for the hierarchial and contemplative life. It must be cleansed from concupiscence, from malice, from ignorance, from infirmity or impotence. Fear

[17] Jerome, *Epistle* 82 (alias 62), 11.
[18] Wisd. 7:11.

brings about the first, piety the second, knowledge the third, fortitude the fourth. For illumination we depend on the acts of reparation and of our original state; counsel gives the first, understanding the second. Perfection must be obtained through attaining the highest good which consists in the One, and this comes through the gift of wisdom: and so the ark of contemplation is finished in breadth, as it were, in a cubit.

9. Seventh and lastly, there ought to be seven gifts of the Holy Ghost to expedite action and contemplation. There ought to be three assisting gifts for contemplation because of the soul's turning to the Trinity; fear for the reverence of authority, understanding for the understanding of truth, and wisdom for the relish of and appetite for goodness. For the active power which is occupied in performing and sustaining, we ought to have four gifts, namely, piety for doing and fortitude for sustaining, and two for their direction, namely, knowledge and counsel. Because direction is necessary for advancement, there is a combination of gifts, and there are many gifts directed to understanding because the light of understanding is a powerful aid in directing our feet in the right path.

CHAPTER SIX

THE DIVISION OF GRACE INTO THE HABITS OF THE BEATITUDES AND CONSEQUENTLY INTO THE HABITS OF BENEFITS AND SENSES

1. On the division of grace into the habits of beatitudes, this must be held: that there are seven beatitudes which the Savior mentioned in the Sermon on the Mount,[19] namely, poverty of spirit, meekness, mourning, hunger after justice, mercy, cleanness of heart, and peace. To these beatitudes, because of their own perfection and fitness, the twelve benefits of the

19 Matt. 5:3 ff.; Gal. 5:22 ff.

Spirit and five spiritual senses are added. These are not called new habits but states of enjoyment and uses of the spiritual knowledge by which the souls of just men are replenished and consoled.

2. The explanation of this is as follows: Since the restorative principle is most perfect and most perfectly restorative and reformative through a gratuitous gift, the gift of grace which flows from it liberally and copiously ought to be divided into habits of perfections. Since these approximate our end, they are rightly called by the name of beatitudes, and their sufficiency, number, and order are derived from the integrity of perfection, from the modes of perfection, and from the dispositions to perfection.

3. First, for the fullness of perfection a complete withdrawal from evil is necessarily required, then a perfect progression in good and a perfect repose in the best. Because evil either proceeds from the swelling of pride, from the rancor of malice, or from the languor of concupiscence, three beatitudes are necessary for the complete withdrawal from this threefold source of evil, namely, poverty of spirit for the evil of swelling, meekness for the evil of rancor, and mourning for the evil of passion and the languor of concupiscence. Because the perfect progression in good is achieved by imitating the divine, and "all the ways of the Lord are mercy and truth." [20] There are two beatitudes for these purposes: hunger or zeal for justice and love of mercy. Because a repose in the best comes either through a clear understanding or through a calm love, there are two ultimate beatitudes, namely, cleanness of heart for the sight of God, and peace of mind for the perfect enjoyment of God.

4. Second, if we consider the modes of perfection, there ought to be seven habits of beatitudes. There is the perfection of religion, of manifestation, and of internal sanctity. For the perfection of religion we need: the renunciation of private

[20] Ps. 24:10.

good, the acceptance of fraternal good, and the desire for eternal good. The first comes through poverty of spirit, the second through the meekness of love, the third through the bitterness of mourning. For the perfection of manifestation two beatitudes are necessary, namely, zeal for justice and love of mercy, for "mercy and truth preserve the king." [21] Accordingly a rule of manifestation ought to be followed in the Church militant. For the perfection of internal sanctity we need purity of conscience and calmness of the whole soul through the peace of God which surpasses all human experience.

5. Third, seven beatitudes are necessary if preceding dispositions are considered. Fear makes one recede from evil and from the occasion of evil. Because the root of all evil is envy,[22] fear disposes one for poverty of spirit, and in this state humility is immediately joined with poverty so that a perfect man is drawn away from the fountain of all fault, namely, from pride and envy. Hence poverty of spirit is the foundation of all evangelical perfection. Hence one who wishes to reach the peak of perfection ought first to lay this foundation, according to the nineteenth chapter of Matthew, "If thou wish to be perfect, go sell what thou hast"; behold perfect poverty which holds nothing back for itself; "and come follow Me." [23] Behold humility, which makes man, by denying himself, bear his cross and follow Christ who is the true foundation of all perfection. Therefore fear disposes one for poverty of spirit. Piety disposes one for meekness, for he who treats anyone piously neither angers him nor is angered by him. Knowledge disposes one for mourning, because through knowledge we learn that we were driven from the state of happiness into this vale of sorrow and tears. Fortitude disposes one for hunger after justice, for he who is brave binds himself so avidly

---

21 Prov. 20:28.
22 I Tim. 6:10.
23 Matt. 19:21.

to justice that he chooses to be separated from life on earth rather than from justice. Counsel disposes one for mercy, for God counsels nothing more strongly in Scripture than to have mercy, which He holds above all sacrifices.[24] Knowledge disposes one for cleanness of heart, for perception of truth cleanses our heart from all phantasies. Wisdom disposes one for peace because wisdom joins us with the highest truth and good, and therein lies the end and rest of our entire rational appetite.

After we have acquired this peace, a superabundant spiritual delight necessarily follows, and this is contained in twelve benefits designed for enjoying the superabundance of delights. Twelve is an abundant number and it includes the abundance of spiritual delights in which the sanctified soul takes pleasure and delight. Man is made ready for contemplation and for the gazes and embraces of groom and bride, understanding these things in their spiritual senses by which the supreme beauty of the groom, Christ, is seen by the power of splendor, the supreme harmony is heard by the power of the Word, the greatest sweetness is tasted by the power of wisdom comprehending both truth and splendor, the greatest fragrance is perceived by the power of the inspired Word in the heart, the greatest sweetness is condensed by the power of the incarnate Word who lives among us bodily and restores Himself to us palpably with a kiss and an embrace in most ardent love which causes the passage of our mind through ecstasy and rapture from this world to the Father.

6. From this discussion it is manifest that the habits of the virtues dispose one principally to the active life, but the habits of the gifts for the quiet of the contemplative way, and the habits of the beatitudes for the perfection of both. The benefits of the spirit (charity, joy, peace, patience, benignity, goodness, long-suffering, mildness, fidelity, modesty, continency, and chastity) bespeak the delights which follow upon perfect deeds. But the spiritual senses bespeak mental perceptions

[24] *Ibid.*, 9:13; 12:7.

about the contemplation of truth. This same contemplation was possessed by the prophets through revelation according to a threefold vision, namely, of the body, of the imagination, and of the intellect. It is found in other just people through speculation which begins in the senses and travels to the imagination, from the imagination to the reason, from the reason to the intellect, from the intellect to the understanding, and from the understanding to wisdom, the highest perception, which begins in this life but is completed in everlasting glory.

7. Jacob's ladder is based on these stages, the top reaching heaven,[25] and so is Solomon's throne[26] on which sits the most wise and truly peaceful King, lovable as a most precious spouse and wholly desirable, upon whom the angels desired to look and for whom the love of holy souls sighs just as the stag seeks fountains of water. Accordingly, by a fervent desire like fire our spirit is made ready for the ascent but with a certain learned ignorance is carried beyond its own self into darkness and delight so that it not only says with the bride: "We will run after thee to the odor of thy ointments,"[27] but also sings with the prophet: "and night shall be my light in my pleasures."[28] No one knows this nocturnal and delightful illumination unless he tries it, and no one tries it except through grace divinely given; and it is given to none except those who train themselves for it. The practices for merit must therefore be considered next.

25 Gen. 28:12.
26 III Kings 10:18 ff. Also referred to in this paragraph: Cant. 5:16; I Pet. 1:12; Ps. 41:1.
27 Cant. 1:3.
28 Ps. 138:11.

CHAPTER SEVEN

THE PRACTICE OF GRACE IN REGARD TO WHAT IS TO BE BELIEVED

1. Fourth, we must consider grace as regards the practices for merit. Concerning these, four things must be considered: first, the practice of grace in regard to what is to be believed, and such are the articles of faith; second, in regard to what is to be loved, and such are those things which look to the order of love; third, in regard to what is to be followed, and such are the precepts of the divine law; fourth, in regard to what is to be asked, and such are the petitions of the Lord's Prayer.

2. As to the articles of faith, we must hold these truths: that, though we are bound to believe through faith all matters which are above reason and, in general, all those matters which are contained and alleged in the canon of Holy Scripture, yet in a particular and proper sense the articles of faith are said to be those which are listed in the enumeration of the Apostles' Creed. These articles in one sense are twelve in number if emphasis is placed upon those who promulgated the Creed, in another sense fourteen if we consider what must definitely be believed as the foundation of all belief.

3. The explanation of this is as follows: Since the first principle is in Himself true and good in the highest degree and in His own work is also just and merciful in the highest degree, and since there ought to be a firm assent to truth in the highest degree, a warm desire for good in the highest degree, a universal subjection to justice in the highest degree, and a confident invocation of mercy in the highest degree and since grace is the consecration of our mind to the service we owe the first principle, hence grace itself chooses and regulates the practices which are due and meritorious as regards what is to be believed, loved, followed, and asked for accord-

ing to what the highest truth, goodness, justice, and mercy in the Blessed Trinity require.

4. Because truth must be believed and greater truth must be believed more, and the greatest truth must be believed most, and the truth of the first principle is infinitely greater than all created truth and more brilliant than all the brilliance of our intellect, it follows that, for our intellect to be well ordered in what is to be believed, it must have more faith in the highest truth than in itself and it must reconcile itself with the worship of Christ and in this way not only believe what is in accord with reason but also what is beyond reason and contrary to sensual experience. If our intellect refuses to do this, it does not show the proper reverence due the greatest truth by preferring its own judgment to the dictates of eternal light because it cannot forego the swelling of pride and unworthy elation.

5. Again, because truth above reason or beyond reason is not evident or apparent truth but is more obscure and most difficult to believe, the demonstration of truth elevating the soul and the testimony of authority confirming the soul are necessary so that truth may be believed more firmly. The first is obtained through infused faith, the second through the authority of Scripture, and both of these come from the highest truth through Jesus Christ, who is Splendor and the Word, and through the Holy Ghost who manifests truth and teaches and makes one believe certainly. Thus it is that authority offers support to faith, and faith assents to authority. Because authority is found principally in Holy Scripture which has been compiled entirely through the Holy Ghost for the determination of catholic faith, true faith does not differ from the Scripture but confirms it in a genuine agreement.

6. Lastly, because the truth which we are directed to believe through faith and with which Holy Scripture concerns itself principally is not any kind of truth, but is divine truth, or such truth as is joined to nature—for in the investigation

of such truth you dwell upon both the reward of the fatherland and the merit of this life—it follows that the articles of faith which are the foundations of faith look either to divinity or to humanity. And since divinity is to be considered as found in three persons, namely, the begetting Father, the begotten Son, and the Holy Ghost proceeding, and in a fourfold operation, namely, creation into being of nature, re-creation into being of grace, resuscitation in the restoration of life, and glorification in the attainment of glory, it follows that there are seven articles concerned with divinity. Similarly, because the humanity of Christ is to be considered as conceived by the Holy Ghost, born of the Virgin, suffering on the cross, descending into hell, rising from the dead, ascending into heaven, and coming for final judgment, it follows that there are seven articles dealing with His humanity. Thus in all there are fourteen articles after the manner of the seven stars and seven candlesticks of gold in the midst of which the Son of man continuously moves.[29]

7. Because Christ is one with a human and divine nature and because the highest truth is one and it is the one, primary, highest, and sole reason for belief which does not change through time, hence despite all the above-mentioned articles there is only one faith, unchangeable in the present, past, and future, although that faith is more clear and explicit to those who come after Christ than to those who preceded His coming, just as the New Testament is clearer than the Old but in both the aforenamed articles are contained.

8. And because the Holy Ghost has joined all these articles of faith contained in the solemn Scriptures into one through the twelve apostles as most trustworthy witnesses, the aforenamed articles have been collected into one Apostles' Creed. Therefore the articles can be called twelve because that is the number of the apostles who composed them, and each apostle has placed into the artifice of faith an article like a living

[29] Apoc. 1:12–16.

stone, and the Holy Ghost correctly foreshadowed this—twelve men who took twelve stones from the bed of the river Jordan for the construction of an altar for the Lord.[30]

CHAPTER EIGHT

THE PRACTICE OF GRACE IN REGARD TO WHAT IS TO BE LOVED

1. As to what is to be loved, this must be held: that, although all divine works are very good, yet four [31] ought properly to be loved out of charity, namely, the eternal God, that which we are, our neighbor, and our body. In our love of these, an order and mode must be observed so that God be loved first and above all and because of Himself; second, that which we are under God and for God; third, our neighbor as ourselves; fourth, our body beneath us and beneath our neighbor as a less important good. For this purpose one infused virtue of love and a twofold command are given, and in this command is found the summation of the Law and of the Prophets, not only as regards the Old Testament but also as regards the New.

2. The explanation of this is as follows: The first principle by the very fact that it is first is the highest, and because it is the highest it is the greatest good, and because it is the greatest good it is supremely blessed and supremely beatific, and because it is supremely beatific it is supremely enjoyable, and because it is supremely enjoyable it must be supremely clung to through love and must be our final place of rest. Because a right and orderly love, called charity, hastens one mainly to that good which it enjoys and in which it rests, and it is itself our reason for loving, it follows that that love is espe-

[30] Jos. 4:2 ff.
[31] Augustine, *De doctrina christiana*, XXIII, 22.

cially loved as leading to happiness, and all other things are loved which through it are suitable for happiness. Since our neighbor was born for happiness just as we have been, and our body was born for happiness with our soul, only four things ought to be loved out of charity, namely, God and our neighbor, our soul and our body.

3. Again, because God is above us as the supreme good, our spirit within us as the intrinsic good, our neighbor next to us as the cognate good, and our body beneath us as the subjected good, this order must be observed in loving: God is loved first and above all things and because of Himself; second, our spirit after God but before every transitory good; third, our neighbor as ourself as a similar good; fourth, our body beneath us as the least good, and the body of our neighbor ought to be kept in the same class because each holds the rank of an inferior good with respect to our spirit.

4. Lastly, because love is an inclination of the mind and the origin of all mental affection and is easily turned toward oneself and with difficulty directed toward one's neighbor and with more difficulty raised to God, it follows that, although four things ought to be loved out of charity, yet only two commandments are given: the one which directs our love toward God, and the second which directs it toward our neighbor.

5. And because precepts refer either to God or our neighbor, alike to the end and that intended for the end, all the commandments and the sum of all the Scriptures are stated in these two commandments. Charity itself is the root, form, and end of the virtues; joining all with the ultimate end and binding all together at once and in order. Hence charity is itself the weight of an ordered inclination and the bond of perfect conjunction preserving order in diverse things that ought to be loved, as regards what is loved and what is achieved, but possessing a unity in the infused virtue as regards the one end and the one primary delight which is the explanation for

loving all other things which are born to be bound together through the band of love into one Christ in head and body, who contains in Himself the total of those to be saved. This unity is begun in this life but is consummated in eternal glory in accordance with the prayer of the Lord, "that they may be one as We also are one: I in them, and Thou in Me: that they may be made perfect in one." [32] When this unity is achieved through the bond of love, God will be all things in all things with certain eternity and perfect peace, and all things will be united through love, ordered in communion, united in order, and indissolubly bound together in union.

CHAPTER NINE

THE PRACTICE OF GRACE AS REGARDS THE OBSERVING OF PRECEPTS AND COUNSELS

1. As to the precepts of the divine law we must hold these truths: that in the Mosaic law there are judicial, figurative, and moral precepts, namely, the ten precepts of the decalogue written on two tables by the finger of God. The Gospel law tempers the judicial by elevating it, cancels the figurative by supplanting it, completes the moral by giving it direction. The Gospels give direction by instructive discussions, and by stimulating promises, and by perfecting counsels, such as the counsels of poverty, obedience, and chastity. Christ our Lord invites him who wishes to be perfect to follow these.

2. The explanation of this is as follows: Just as the first principle is the highest good in itself, so it has the highest justice in directing its own work and in governing the universe. Because a man who is most just longs for justice not only for himself but for his neighbor, and justice consists in conforming oneself to the rules of law, hence divine justice should state

[32] John 17:22.

and explain the rules of justice to man, not only by teaching through an explanation of the truth, but by giving precepts and making them obligatory through commanding the will. Since grace makes our will conform to the divine will, it is the part of grace to dispose us to obey and submit to those rules of justice according to the law divinely given.

3. Again, since obedience to the divine commands occurs in two ways, namely, from fear of punishment or from love of justice, and the first is for the imperfect and the second for the perfect, God gave a twofold law to man: one of fear and one of love; one begetting servitude, the other bringing about our adoption as children of God.[33] Because it is suitable that the fearful and the imperfect be frightened through judgments, guided through signs, and directed through precepts, the Mosaic law, which is the law of fear, contains the judicial, figurative, and moral. For the perfect and the loving there are suited the plain teaching of the Gospels, the generous promise of rewards, and the high perfection of the counsels. Thus it is that the Gospel law contains these three. Hence the Mosaic law is said to differ from the Gospel law because the former is the law of figure, the latter of truth; the former the law of punishment, the latter of grace; the former literal, the latter spiritual; the former destroying, the latter vivifying; the former of fear, the latter of love; the former of servitude, the latter of liberty; the former of burden, the latter of facility.

4. Lastly, because the rules adapted to the necessity of justice are contained in the divine precepts, and justice is "to render to everyone his due," [34] there must be moral precepts which bring us in line with God, and others which bring us in line with our neighbor according to the twofold precept of charity which the Holy Ghost has chosen to put into everyone's bosom through the mystery of the two tablets, said to

[33] Rom. 8:15; Gal. 4:24 ff.
[34] Plato, *Dialogus de republica,* I; Aristotle, *Ethics,* V, 1.

have been written by the finger of God. Because God is triune, namely, Father, Son, and Holy Ghost, whose majesty deserves to be adored, whose truth ought to be acknowledged, and whose love deserves to be accepted, in accord with the irascible, rational, and concupiscible power, in deed, woid, and heart, hence there is a threefold commandment on the first tablet, corresponding to the three aforementioned, namely, submissive adoration, truthful oath-taking, and sacred observance of the Sabbath.

5. Because our neighbor is an image of the Trinity and piety is due him in proportion as he bears the image of the Father, truth in proportion as he bears the image of the Son, and kindness in proportion as he bears the image of the Spirit, there are seven commandments on the second tablet. In regard to piety there are two: one which orders piety, namely, honoring one's father, the other which forbids impiety, namely, forbidding murder. In regard to veracity, which exists mainly in the word, one commandment is given, namely, forbidding lying. In regard to kindness, which is opposed by avarice and concupiscence, both of which can exist in deed or in the heart, four commandments are given, namely, thou shalt not commit adultery, thou shalt not covet thy neighbor's wife, thou shalt not steal, and thou shalt not covet thy neighbor's goods.[35] These have to be arranged according to their greater or lesser wickedness as they impair justice. Thus the rules adapted to the necessity of justice ought to be contained in ten commandments.

6. Because justice reaches perfection when man separates himself completely from evil both from sin and from its cause, and all evil springs from a threefold root, namely, concupiscence of the flesh, concupiscence of the eyes, and the pride of life; hence there are three evangelical counsels which separate us completely from the above-mentioned threefold root. They are counsels because, as they constitute a perfect separation

[35] Exod. 20:12 ff.; Deut. 5:18 ff.

from evil, not only do they separate us from illicit acts but also from licit and allowed acts which can be an occasion of evil. Hence not only do they contain the minimum of justice but also abundant justice to satisfy the demands of perfection of the Gospel law and the arousing of perfecting grace.

CHAPTER TEN

THE PRACTICE OF GRACE AS REGARDS PETITION AND PRAYER

1. On the subject of the petitions of the Lord's Prayer, we must hold that, although God is most liberal and more prepared to give than we are to receive, yet He wishes to receive prayers from us so that He may have occasion to increase the gifts of grace of the Holy Ghost. He wishes to receive not only mental prayer, which is "the raising of the mind to God," but also verbal prayer, which is the "petition for the things that are fitting from God." [36] He wishes prayers not only from us but through the saints, who are helpers divinely given to us so that we may be able to petition through the saints for what we are less worthy to petition ourselves. Because we do not know what we should pray and lest we wander aimlessly, He has given us the form in a prayer which He composed. The sum total of what we should petition is included in the seven petitions of this prayer.

2. The explanation of this is as follows: Just as the first principle is the highest truth and good in itself, so He is merciful and just in His deeds. And because the first principle is most merciful, He must freely mitigate human misery through the infusion of His grace. But because He is at the same time just, He does not give a perfect gift except to one who wishes it, He does not give grace except to him who is thankful, He

[36] John Damascene, *De fide orthodoxa*, III, 24.

does not offer mercy except to him who knows misery, so that man's freedom of choice may be preserved and that the excellence of the gift may not assume trifling value and that the respect for the divine honor may persist unimpaired. Because the petitioner must solicit divine aid, allege his own weakness, and give thanks for the benefit freely given, prayer disposes one for the reception of divine gifts, and God wishes to be prayed to so that He may increase His dispensation of gifts.

3. Again, because our affection must be earnest, our meditation concentrated on one thing, and our hope certain and firm in order for our desire to rise effectively for divine gifts and because our heart is frequently lukewarm, frequently spread over many things, even frequently timid because of the remorse of sin, and does not dare of itself to be seen before the divine countenance, the Lord wished us not only to pray mentally but also to pray verbally to arouse our affection through words. He also wished us to petition through the saints, and the saints in behalf of us to give confidence to the timid so that those who do not dare or are not able to pray by themselves may succeed through suitable petitioners. In this way humility will be preserved in those praying, dignity manifested in the intercessions of the saints, and love and unity shown in all the members of Christ, by which all things which are inferior may confidently seek the superior, and the superior may freely put themselves at the disposal of the inferior.

4. Lastly, because a just and merciful God ought not to listen except to those prayers directed to His honor and to our salvation, and such are prayers which have reference to the reward of the fatherland and the needs of this life, and of the former there are three, of the latter four, hence the petitions of the Lord's Prayer which teach us what we should usefully petition are seven.[37] Those petitions referring to divine honor and the reward of the fatherland are three, namely, understanding of truth, reverence for sovereignty, and harmony of

[37] Matt. 6:9 ff.; Luke 11:2 ff.

will, or in other words: (1) the vision of the greatest truth which only the pure and the holy see and which we seek when we say, "Hallowed be Thy name," that is, that knowledge of Thy name may be given to the perfect, pious, and pure; (2) the exertion of the greatest effort which makes kings and through which we attain the kingdom, and this we seek when we say, "Thy kingdom come"; and (3) the achievement of the highest good which is only for those who have brought their wills into conformity with the divine will, and this we seek when we say, "Thy will be done on earth as it is in heaven." Then follow the petitions which refer to our journey in this life, and they are directed either to the gaining of helpful good or the removal of harmful evil. The gaining of helpful good is sought in the daily or supersubstantial bread in which we seek whatever is necessary for the preservation of the present life either for soul or for body. The removal of harmful evil is sought in the three final petitions because all evil clings to us in the past, present, and future, or in other words, we retain traces of the commission of evil, of the battle with evil, or of the punishment for evil. The petitioner seeks the removal of the first in the forgiveness of trespasses, of the second in victory over temptations, and of the third and last in the delivery from the oppression of evil. Thus there are in all seven petitions which seek all that we should ask. This sufficiently demonstrates that the group of seven petitions corresponds to the group of seven divine graces and gifts of a sevenfold grace.

5. Therefore we should note that Holy Scripture offers us for our consideration the sevenfold set of sevenfolds, namely, the capital sins, the sacraments, the virtues, the gifts, the beatitudes, the petitions, and the dowries of glory, three spiritual and four corporeal, as will be seen later.[38] Holy Scripture describes first, the group of seven sins from which we must withdraw; secondly, the group of seven sacraments through which we must advance; lastly, the group of seven dowries for which

[38] Cf. *infra*, Part VII, chap. 7.

we must seek; next to the last, the group of seven petitions with which we must seek; and the groups of seven virtues, gifts, and beatitudes, a threefold intermediate through which we ought to advance. Thus praising the name of the Lord and praying seven times a day, we may implore the sevenfold grace of the virtues, gifts, and beatitudes by which grace we shall conquer in the sevenfold battle with the capital sins and proceed to the sevenfold crown of glorious dowries with the aid of the sevenfold remedy of the sacraments divinely designed for the restoration of the human race.

PART SIX

THE SACRAMENTAL REMEDY

CHAPTER ONE

THE ORIGIN OF THE SACRAMENTS

1. After the treatise on the Trinity of God, the creation of the universe, the corruption of sin, the incarnation of the Word, and the grace of the Holy Ghost, we must now, in the sixth place, consider the sacramental remedy. In this treatment seven things must be considered: the origin of the sacraments, their variety, distinction, institution, dispensation, repetition, and especially the integrity of each.

2. As to the origin of the sacraments, we must hold that they are sensible signs divinely instituted as remedies, in which "under the covering of sensible things a divine power secretly operates," [1] so that "they represent by similitude, signify by their institution, and confer a certain spiritual grace by sanctification" through which the soul is cured from the infirmities of vices. They are chiefly designed with this as their ultimate end. They also promote humility, instruction, and virtuous deeds as their secondary end.

3. The explanation of this is as follows: Because the restorative principle, which is Christ crucified, namely, the incarnate Word, who takes care of all things most wisely, is divine and cures most mercifully because He is divinely incarnate, He ought to restore and heal the ailing human race in a manner suitable to the one ailing, the sickness, the occasion of his becoming sick, and the cure of the sickness itself. That physician is the incarnate Word, the invisible God in visible nature. Ailing man is not spirit alone or flesh alone, but spirit in mortal flesh. The sickness is original sin which through ig-

[1] Isidore of Seville, *Etymologia*, XIX, 10.

norance poisons the mind and through concupiscence the flesh. Although the origin of this fault is principally in the consent of the reason, yet it has its occasion in the senses of the flesh. In order that the remedy may correspond to all the above-mentioned, not only must it be spiritual, but it must possess something in the way of a sensible sign, so that, as sensible signs were the occasion of the fall of the soul, so they may be the occasion of its resurrection. Because sensible signs considered in themselves do not possess an efficacious tendency toward grace although they bear a remote representation of grace in their own nature, the signs should be instituted for signification and blessed for sanctification by the Author of grace that thus they may represent by a natural similitude, signify by the institution associated with them, sanctify by superadded blessing, and prepare for grace which heals and cures our soul.

4. Again, because curative grace is not given to the proud, to the unbelieving, and to the disdainful, the sensible signs ought to be given divinely not only to sanctify and confer grace and through this process heal, but also to instruct through their signification, to humble by their reception, and to lead to virtue by their diversity. And this so that when the tendency to slip has been removed from the concupiscible through practice, when ignorance has been removed from the rational through instruction, and when pride has been removed from the irascible through humility, the whole soul may become susceptible of cure by the grace of the Holy Ghost which restores us in respect to these three powers to the image of the Trinity and of Christ.

5. Lastly, because through such sensible signs the divinely instituted grace of the Holy Ghost is received and is discovered in them by those to whom they are presented, the sacraments are called the vessel of grace [2] and the cause of grace. This is so not because grace is contained substantially in them

2 Hugh of St. Victor, *De sacramentis*, XIX, 10.

or effected causally by them,[3] since it can be made to reside in the soul alone and can be infused by God alone, but because in them and through them the grace for our cure ought to be infused by the great physician, Christ, by divine decree, "although God does not bind His power in the sacraments" (Peter Lombard, *Quattuor libri sententiarum*, IV, 1, 5).

6. From what has been said above it is apparent not only what the origin of the sacraments is but what their use is and what their results are. Their origin is Christ the Lord; their use is their practice, their instruction, and their humiliation; and their result is the cure and salvation of men. It is also clear that the efficient cause of the sacraments is their divine institution, that their material cause is their representation by a sensible sign, that their formal cause is sanctifying grace, and that their final cause is the cure of man. Because "a name comes from the form and from the end," [4] they are called sacraments, as it were, sanctifying remedies. Through them the soul is led from the baseness of sin back to perfect sanctification. Therefore, although the sacraments are corporeal and sensible, they are venerated as sacred because they signify sacred mysteries, prepare for sacred gifts, are given by the most sacred God, are divinely consecrated by a sacred institution and blessing, and are dedicated to the most sacred worship of God in His sacred Church. Thus they deservedly ought to be called sacraments.

CHAPTER TWO

THE VARIETY OF THE SACRAMENTS

1. As to the variety of the sacraments we must hold that the sacraments were instituted from the very beginning for the cure of man and always are concurrent with the sickness

[3] St. Bonaventure may seem here to be denying any causality to the sacraments. Modern theologians clearly recognize that the sacraments have causality.
[4] Aristotle, *De anima*, II, 4.

of man and will continue to the end of the world. Some sacraments existed in the law of nature, some under the written law, others under grace. In all these types those which came later are more evident in their meaning and more worthy in their effect as to grace. In the law of nature there were oblations, sacrifices, and tithes. In the written law, however, circumcision was introduced, atonement was added, and many kinds of offerings, tithes, and sacrifices were introduced. In the new law, moreover, "sacraments fewer in number, more potent in usefulness and more efficacious in virtue were established," [5] and they are more worthy of pre-eminence. In them lies the fulfillment and at the same time the voiding of all the sacraments above mentioned.

2. The explanation of this is as follows: The incarnate Word, who is the principle of our reparation and the fount and origin of the sacraments, since He is most merciful and most wise, does not, in so far as He is most clement, permit the sickness of sin to continue without the remedy of a sacrament; and in so far as He is most wise, He has, according to the dictates of His immutable wisdom which governs all things in a most orderly way, devised remedies which are different and vary according to the corresponding changes of time. Because "from the beginning, with the advance of time and with the advent of the Savior drawing closer and closer, the effect of salvation increased more and more and the understanding of truth likewise, it was fitting both that the signs of salvation themselves should be varied, some succeeding others as the times changed so that the effect of divine grace in salvation should increase, and that the meaning of the visible signs should at the same time become more evident." [6] Therefore, "first through oblation and afterwards through circumcision and lastly through the baptismal cleansing, the sacrament of expiation and sanctification was instituted, because the form

[5] Augustine, *Contra Faustum*, IX, 13.
[6] Hugh of St. Victor, *op. cit.*, I, 9, 6.

and likeness of that cleansing is found in the oblation in a hidden way, in the circumcision it is expressed more clearly, and through baptism it is shown more manifestly." [7] Hence "these sacraments of the early time," as Hugh says,[8] "were like a shadow of truth, in the intermediate time like a figure or image of truth, and those in the last time, namely, in the time of grace, are as the body of truth" because within them they contain truth and curing grace which they offer and they presently confer what they promise.

3. Again, because the presence of truth and grace which is clear in the law of grace could not be expressed in one sign as was fitting by reason of an excellence, multiformity in operation and power, it follows that in every age and law many sacraments were given to elicit that truth and grace but especially in the time of the law of figure, whose function it was to represent in figure, many varied signs existed and by their variety they expressed in a multiform way the grace of Christ and commended it more excellently and by commending it in a multiple way nourished the little ones and practiced the imperfect and by weighing down the hardened broke down their resistance and accustomed them to the yoke of grace and in a certain way softened them.

4. Lastly, because by the coming of truth the shadow ceases and the foreshadowing figure attains its intended end, its use and activity ought thereupon to cease; hence by the coming of grace the old sacraments and signs are likewise fulfilled and cease, since signs prognosticated and, as it were, foretold what was far away, and the new sacraments were instituted as demonstrative of the present grace and as a kind of remembrance of the passion of our Lord who is the fountain and origin of curative grace either in us or in those who preceded the coming of Christ: in those who preceded as a promised reward, in those who follow as an achieved reward.

[7] *Ibid.*
[8] *Ibid.*

Because grace is not owing for a promised reward unless the reward is achieved, and grace is owing more abundantly in the case of achieved reward than in the promised one, it follows that the passion of Christ more immediately sanctifies the sacraments of the time of the new law and grace resides in them more fully. For that reason the old sacraments prepared for and led to the new as a path leads to its end, as the sign leads to what it signifies, as the figure leads to truth, and as the imperfect leads to and prepares for the perfect.

CHAPTER THREE

THE NUMBER AND DISTINCTION OF THE SACRAMENTS

1. As to the distinction and number of sacraments under the new law, this must be held: They are seven in number, corresponding to the sevenfold form of grace, which through the seven periods of time leads us back to the principle, rest, and circle of eternity, as it also leads to the eighth age of universal resurrection. Baptism is the door opening the way to these sacraments; then follow confirmation, Holy Eucharist, penance, extreme unction, holy orders, and matrimony. Although matrimony is placed last because of the sickness of concupiscence joined with it, nevertheless it was introduced in Paradise before all the others, even before sin.

2. The explanation of this is as follows: Our principle of restoration, Christ, the Lord, the incarnate Word, since He is the power and wisdom of God and our mercy,[9] ought to institute the sacraments in the law of grace so powerfully, so wisely, so mercifully, and so fittingly that absolutely nothing should be wanting for our cure as regards what belongs to our present state of life. These three are necessary for the per-

9 I Cor. 1:24.

fect cure of sickness: the removal of sickness, the infusion of health, and the preservation of the infused health. As to the first, because a perfect and complete removal of sickness is required for a perfect cure and because sickness is sevenfold (threefold as regards fault, namely, original, mortal, and venial fault, and fourfold as regards the result of fault, namely, ignorance, malice, weakness, and concupiscence), and "that which cures the heel does not cure the eye," as Jerome says,[10] it is proper that this group of seven remedies be directed to more fully removing the sevenfold sickness, namely, baptism against original fault, penance against mortal fault, extreme unction against venial fault, holy orders against ignorance, the Eucharist against malice, confirmation against weakness, and matrimony against the concupiscence it tempers and excuses.

3. Again, because the perfect cure cannot exist without the restoration of complete health, and the complete health of the soul consists·in the use of the seven virtues, namely, the three theological and the four cardinal, the group of seven sacraments was properly instituted to restore the healthy use of these virtues. Baptism restores one to health and disposes one for faith, confirmation for hope, the Eucharist for charity, penance for justice, extreme unction for perseverance which is the complement and summation of bravery, holy orders for prudence, and matrimony for the preservation of temperance which the weakness of our flesh particularly needs but the righteousness of marriage remedies.

4. Lastly, because the perfect cure cannot exist without preservation of the infused health and because infused health cannot be preserved in the conflict of battle except in the ranks of the Church and its ranks are as terrifying as the well-ordered ranks of an army; and because this is due to the armor of the sevenfold grace, there must be seven sacraments. In order that the ranks may be perfectly and continually fortified and since they consist of corruptible parts, they need fortifying, strength-

10 Jerome, *Commentarius in Marcum*, IX, 28.

ening, and restoring sacraments: the fortifying sacraments for those in battle, the strengthening sacraments for those falling, and the restoring sacraments for those dying. The fortifying sacraments fortify either the recruits through baptism or the veterans through confirmation or the departing ones through extreme unction. The strengthening sacraments either help us rise from a venial fall through Holy Eucharist or from a mortal fall through penance. The restorative sacraments either restore the spiritual being through orders whose duty it is to administer the sacraments or restore the natural being through matrimony which, because it secures the multiplication of beings in nature, the foundation of all, was introduced first before all the others. But because the sickness of concupiscence is connected with matrimony and because it sanctifies the least, although it is a great sacrament in meaning, it is placed last among the spiritual remedies. Hence because baptism is for the recruits, confirmation for those in battle, the Eucharist for those regaining their strength, penance for those that are rising, extreme unction for those departing, orders for the introduction of new soldiers, and matrimony for the creation of new soldiers, we understand the sufficiency and order of the sacramental remedies and arms.

CHAPTER FOUR

THE INSTITUTION OF THE SACRAMENTS

1. As to the institution of the sacraments, this must be held: that the seven sacraments of the law of grace were instituted by Christ, the mediator of the New Testament and the principal proposer of the law in which He has invited us to the things eternally promised, given us guiding precepts, and instituted the sanctifying sacraments. He has instituted the sacraments in words and principles for clearness of meaning and efficacy of sanctification so that they always signify truth but do not always effect a cure, not because of a defect

on their part, but because of a defect on the part of the receiver. He instituted the above-mentioned sacraments for different reasons: some of them confirming, sanctioning, and consummating, as matrimony and penance, some fortifying and initiating, as confirmation and extreme unction, some initiating and consummating in their reception, as the sacraments of baptism, Eucharist, and holy orders. The last three He Himself fully instituted and was the first to receive.[11]

2. The explanation of this is as follows: Because our restorative principle is the crucified Christ, namely, the incarnate Word, and because the Word, since it is coequal and consubstantial with the Father, has the greatest power, highest truth, and highest goodness, and thus the highest authority, it was proper for Him to introduce the New Testament, to give the entire and sufficient law required by His own highest power, truth, and goodness. By reason of His highest goodness He has offered beatifying gifts, by reason of His highest truth He has given guiding principles, and by reason of His highest power He has instituted the assisting sacraments. This was done so that through the sacraments our power may be restored to enable us to follow the guiding principles, and that through the guiding precepts we may attain the eternal promises made by the eternal Word, namely, the Lord Christ, in the Gospel law, for He is "the way and the truth and the life" (John 14:6).

3. Again, because the restorative principle is not only the Word in so far as He is the Word but also in so far as He is incarnate, who by the very fact that He is incarnate offers Himself to all for understanding truth and shows Himself to all who approach worthily for curative grace, He instituted the sacraments in elements as well as words, as the fullness of grace

---

[11] The use of the word "receive" here (Latin, *suscepit*) is not supported by any of St. Bonaventure's other writings. They do not support a construction of the word "receive" here to mean that Christ went through the ceremony of these sacraments as a recipient. He was baptized by St. John in the Jordan, but in the opinion of modern theologians this was not the sacrament of baptism. Christ also was a priest, but by virtue of His role as mediator in the redemption.

and truth, to manifest more clearly the meaning of the sacraments and to show the efficacy of their sanctification. And that was done so that, while the elements present themselves to the eyes, and the words to the ears—for these are the two senses especially equipped for knowledge—they might convey a clear meaning and the words sanctify the elements so that the efficacy of the human cure might become fuller because the cure is given to no one who has rejected or questioned the fountain of grace within his heart. For these reasons the sacraments were instituted in such a way that they might have meaning universally and forever, but they sanctify only those who approach worthily and free from all guile.

4. Lastly, because, even though the incarnate Word is the fountain of sacramental grace, yet some sacramental grace was in existence before the Incarnation, though some did not exist until after the descent of the Holy Ghost, and some existed in an in-between manner, it was fitting that the sacraments be instituted in a diverse manner. Before the Incarnation both penitential compunction and matrimonial generation were necessary. Hence He did not institute these two sacraments anew but merely completed and confirmed in the Gospel law what had already been instituted by Him and had been established in a certain way by natural decree when He preached penance and was in the midst of those being married, and approved the law of marriage as is gathered from different places in the Gospel.[12] Before the descent of the Holy Ghost there was no complete bestowing of the Holy Ghost in confirmation and no public confession of the name of Christ, nor was there the unction preparing the mind for flight. Therefore Christ alone initiated and brought forth the two sacraments of confirmation and extreme unction: confirmation by imposing His hand on little children and by instructing the disciples to baptize in the Holy Ghost, and extreme unction by sending the disciples to cure the sick, and the disciples

12 Matt. 4:17; Mark 1:14 f.; John 2:1 ff.; Matt. 19:4 ff.

anointed the sick with oil, as is stated in Mark.[13] In the intermediate time there was a regeneration and an ordination of the Church and a spiritual repast. Therefore Christ instituted these three sacraments, namely, baptism, the Eucharist, and orders, all complete and distinct. In the case of baptism He did so first by receiving baptism and then by giving the form and by making it known to others; in the case of orders, by first giving the power of binding and loosing the sins of the human race and the power of confecting the sacrament of the altar; in the case of the Eucharist, by comparing Himself to a grain of wheat and, on the eve of His passion, by confecting the sacrament of His body and blood and giving it to His disciples. Therefore these three sacraments ought to have been instituted distinctly and entirely by Christ and foreshadowed in many ways in the old law, but instituted as substantial sacraments in the New Testament proper to the lawgiver, namely, the incarnate Word.

CHAPTER FIVE

THE DISPENSATION OF THE SACRAMENTS

1. As to the dispensation of the sacraments this must be held: that the power of dispensing the sacraments belongs regularly to the human race alone. In the dispensing of all sacraments, intention in dispensing them is necessary. In some a priest or a bishop is required besides the intention. A bishop is necessary to the dispensation of confirmation and orders, but a priest suffices for the dispensation of the Eucharist, penance, and extreme unction. Baptism and matrimony, though they concern priests, can be performed in fact outside the order of the priesthood, especially in the face of necessity. In these cases the sacraments can be performed by the good and

[13] Mark 6:13; 10:13; Luke 18:15; Acts 1:5.

by the bad, by the faithful and by the heretic, within the Church and outside: within the Church according to truth and to advantage in grace, but outside not to advantage but only according to truth.

2. The explanation of this is as follows: Our restorative principle, namely, the incarnate Word, in so far as He is God and man, instituted the sacraments for the welfare of men and ordained, as was indeed fitting, that they may be performed for men through the agency of men to preserve the conformity of the dispenser to the Savior Christ and for the salvation of man himself. Because Christ the Savior saved the human race in conformity with justice, the dignity of order and the certainty of salvation—for He devoted Himself to our salvation in a right, orderly, and certain manner—it follows that for these three reasons He has commissioned the administering of the sacraments to man. First because probity of justice demands that the works of man, in so far as he is man, be not done with headlong haste, and the works of man as a minister of Christ in some way refer back to Christ, and the works of man as minister of salvation in some way refer back to salvation either in general or in particular, and because the dispensation of the sacraments is the work of man as a rational being, as the minister of Christ, and as the minister of salvation, such ministration must be done with an intention and with the intention that the party wishes to do what Christ instituted for human salvation or to do at least what the Church does, for in what the Church does the above-mentioned intention is in a general way included because the Church herself, as she receives the sacraments from Christ, dispenses them for the welfare of the faithful.

3. Again, because the order of worthiness demands that greater things be committed to the greater, lesser to the lesser, and the intermediate to the intermediate, and some sacraments look mainly to excellence in virtue or worthiness, as the sacraments of confirmation and of orders, some reflect a need, as

baptism and matrimony, for the one generates, the other re-
generates to the required existence, and some are intermediate,
as the Eucharist, penance, and extreme unction, it follows that
the first group, which is supreme, cannot be dispensed except
by archbishops and bishops in so far as dispensation comes
under the common law, but the others, which are inferior, can
be dispensed by anyone with orders and even by inferior persons, especially in the face of necessity, as, for example, in the
case of baptism. The intermediate sacraments, however, can
be dispensed by priests alone, who are between bishops and
inferior persons in the middle position.

4. Lastly, because the security of salvation demands that
the sacraments be so dispensed that uncertainty does not arise,
and since there is no one who may be certain of the goodness
and faith of the dispenser, and the recipient cannot even be
certain whether he himself is worthy of love or hate, it follows
that, if the sacraments could be performed by the good alone,
no one would be certain about the reception of the sacrament
and so they would always be repeated. The wickedness of one
would prejudice the salvation of another. The grades of the
hierarchy of the Church militant would lack stability, which
is required for the dispensation of the sacraments. Therefore it was fitting that the dispensation of the sacraments be
committed to man not by reason of sanctity, which varies according to the will, but because of authority, which always remains the same, according to what it is in itself. Hence authority ought to be extended to the good and the bad, to those
who are within and to those who are outside of the Church.
Because outside of the unity of faith and love which makes us
sons and members of the Church, no one can be saved, hence
if the sacraments are received outside the Church, they are
not effective for salvation although they are true sacraments.
However, they can become useful if one returns to Holy
Mother Church, the only spouse of Christ, whose sons alone
Christ the spouse deems worthy of eternal inheritance. Thus

Augustine argues against the Donatists: "The Church compared to Paradise indicates to us that certain men are able to receive her baptism even outside of her, but that no one is able either to grasp or to retain the salvation of beatitude outside of her. The rivers from the font of Paradise, as the Scripture testifies, flowed widely outside. They are remembered by name and it is known to all through what lands they flowed and that they existed outside of Paradise. But the happiness of life mentioned in Paradise existed neither in Mesopotamia nor in Egypt, in which those rivers flowed. So it is that, though the water of Paradise is outside of Paradise, there is no beatitude except within Paradise. So the baptism of the Church can exist outside the Church but the gift of a blessed life is not found except within the Church which was founded on a rock and received the keys of binding and loosing. She is the one that keeps and possesses every power of her spouse and Lord, and through this conjugal power she can also bring forth sons from the handmaids, who, if they be not proud, shall be called into their share of inheritance. If, however, they are proud, they shall remain without. Because we fight for the honor and unity of the Church, let us not concede to the heretics what we know to be false, but rather let us teach them by arguments that they cannot attain salvation from unity unless they attain to that same unity" (Augustine, *De baptismo contra Donatistas,* IV, 1 and 2).

CHAPTER SIX

THE REPETITION OF THE SACRAMENTS

1. As to the repetition of the sacraments, this must be held: that, although it is common to all the sacraments to be repeated neither on the same person and occasion nor for the same reason lest the sacraments be derided, yet three sacra-

ments in particular must not in a certain sense be repeated, namely, baptism, confirmation, and orders. In the reception of these three there is impressed a threefold uneffaceable internal character. The baptismal character constitutes the basis of these, and the others cannot be impressed unless it is impressed first. Thus if an unbaptized person is ordained, nothing is thereby effected, and everything must be redone because "that is not understood as repetition which rests upon that which was not done." [14]

2. The explanation of this is as follows: Our restorative principle, namely, the incarnate Word, who by reason of His most high power, wisdom, and goodness does nothing ineffectively, nothing improperly, and nothing unfruitfully, certainly ought to observe this in His most noble works such as the works by which the human race is redeemed. Because the sacraments are of that type of divine work, there would be a certain dishonor to them when they were repeated on the same occasion and same person and for the same reason, because this shows that they have been dispensed ineffectually, inaptly, and unfruitfully, contrary to what the highest power, wisdom, and goodness of the restorative principle requires, for He always assists and operates in and through the sacraments.

3. Again, because there are some among the restoring sacraments which in general have the efficacy of the divine power for the restoration of the human race and were instituted only to remedy sickness, but others are to institute, distinguish, and set in order the degrees of the hierarchy in the Church—and sickness can be varied, expelled, and introduced again and the degrees of the Church must be firm, solid, and resolute—it follows that the sacraments which care for recurrent sicknesses have transient effects and may be repeated for a new reason. Those sacraments which refer to the degrees of the hierarchy and the distinguishing ranks of the faith must impart besides

---

[14] Innocent III, C. *Veniens* (3) X de presbytero non baptizato (Bk. III, tit. 43); C. *Tuae litterae* (1), X de clerico per saltum promoto (Bk. V, tit. 29).

remedial effects other permanent effects preserving the fixed and stable distinction of degrees and ranks in the Church. Because this cannot be done through natural gifts or through gratuitous gifts *gratum facientia*,[15] it must be done through certain signs indicating an incorruptible substance, namely, an incorruptible soul, through an incorruptible principle in conformity with things that are incorruptibly, ineffaceably, and gratuitously impressed, and these are called characters. Since these characters never can be effaced, they can never be repeated, nor can those sacraments be repeated in which these characters are impressed.

4. Lastly, because there is a threefold status of faith giving rise to a grouping of Christian people in the ranks of the ecclesiastical hierarchy, namely, the status of faith begotten, of that fortified, and of that augmented, and by the first there is the distinction of the faithful from the unbelieving, by the second the distinction of the brave from the infirm and weak, by the third the distinction of the clergy from the laity, it follows that those sacraments reflecting the aforenamed threefold status of faith impress characters and will always be distinguished by these indelible marks and hence they can never be repeated. Because baptism reflects the status of the newborn faith by which the people of God are distinguished from the unbelieving, as the Israelites were from the Egyptians, and because confirmation reflects the status of the fortified faith by which strong people are distinguished from the infirm just as fighters are from those who are not fit for fighting, and because orders reflects the status of the augmented faith by which the clergy is distinguished from the laity as the Levites were from the other tribes, characters are impressed in these three sacraments only.

5. Because the distinction of the people of God from those not of God is first and radical, the baptismal character is the basis of all the other characters. Therefore, when that does

---

[15] See note 2, p. 141, *supra.*

not exist as a foundation, nothing can be built upon it, and hence it is necessary that it be administered anew. If baptism has been received, the others can be impressed, but they can never again be repeated; nor are the three aforenamed sacraments which impress these marks to be repeated for any other cause. A grave punishment must necessarily be placed on those repeating them because of the dishonor shown thereby to a divine sacrament. However, the other four may be repeated for diverse reasons without dishonor to them.

CHAPTER SEVEN

THE CONSTITUTION AND INTEGRITY OF BAPTISM

1. In the seventh place we must consider the integrity of each and every sacrament. Although the sacraments are seven in number, something must first be said about the integrity of baptism, which is the door to the other sacraments.

2. As to the integrity of the sacrament of baptism, this must be held: that for anyone to be baptized truly and completely, the expression of the vocal form instituted by our Lord is required: I baptize thee in the name of the Father and of the Son and of the Holy Ghost. Amen; without the omission of a word and without the insertion of a word; without a disturbance of the above-mentioned order and without a change of the above-mentioned names. An immersion or cleansing of the entire body by water or at least of a more worthy part is also required so that expression and immersion are accomplished by one and the same person and at the same time. By these concurrent actions, if there is no feigning in the baptism, a grace regenerating, rectifying, and purifying from all sin is given. That the grace may become effective, instruction and exercise are given the neophyte, whether child or adult, and

yet, though their own faith is required of adults, faith on the part of another suffices in the case of children.

3. The explanation of this is as follows: Since our restorative principle, namely, the incarnate Word, as the most perfect and sufficient principle, has to restore the human race through the remedies of the sacraments in such a way that nothing is superfluous in the sacraments, nothing irregular, nothing too small, He ought to have so disposed matters that the sacrament of baptism and the others would be integrated according as His power, our salvation, and our sickness demanded. Because the power restoring us is the power of the entire Trinity, which Holy Mother Church believes in her heart, confesses in her word, and professes in her sign, recognizing the distinction, nature, order, and natural origin of the three persons, and because that power is also the power of the passion of Christ who died, was buried, and rose on the third day, it follows that for the expression of all of these in that sacrament, which is the first of all sacraments and in which this power is first and primarily active, there ought to have been an expression of the Trinity in a distinct, proper, and orderly naming, since it is a common form, though in the time of the early Church it could be done in the name of Christ in which the Trinity is understood. There ought to be a proper and orderly recitation of the baptismal words with a triple immersion, if feasible, for the expression of the death of Christ, His burial, and the resurrection He brought about after the third day. Because each power is active at the same time and in one Christ the Savior, both of these acts ought to be done by one and the same person at the same time because unity must be preserved in the sacrament, and unity must be indicated in our Mediator.

4. Again, because our salvation had to be begun through regeneration and revival into being of the grace which confers spiritual being by cleansing impurity, by dissipating darkness, and by chilling the concupiscence falling on every man

descending seminally from Adam, hence the first and regenerative sacrament ought to use the element conforming in its natural representation to the aforenamed threefold effect of the grace which begins our salvation. Because water cleanses by its own purity, is informative by its own permeation of light, and chills with its own coldness, and especially because among all liquids it is common to all mankind, the sacrament of our regeneration ought to use the element of water without a distinction because "all water is in the same species with all water," [16] lest someone's salvation be endangered by the lack of water.

5. Finally, because our sickness, against which baptism is principally directed, is original sin which deprives the soul of the life of grace and the habilitating correctness of all the virtues and renders it in some way prone to every species of sin, and otherwise misleads the soul and "makes a child concupiscible and an adult concupiscent in act," [17] and drives the soul back into diabolical slavery and into the power of the prince of darkness, hence, that a sufficient counteracting remedy may be applied through this sacrament, it was fitting that in that sacrament regenerating grace should be given to counteract the deprivation of the life of grace and also rectifying grace with its sevenfold power against the lack of habilitating virtue and also that grace purifying one from all sin and counteracting the inclination toward the disorder of vice.

6. And because original sin is brought from another source and makes a child concupiscible and an adult concupiscent in act, one's own faith and contrition are necessary in an adult, but another's suffices in a child, namely, that found in the universal Church. Because baptism ought to release children as well as adults from the servitude of the devil and the power of the prince of darkness, both ought to be exorcised, to expunge the opposing power, and both must also be instructed:

[16] Aristotle, *Topica*, I, 6.
[17] Peter Lombard, *Quattuor libri sententiarum*, II, 30, 9.

adults so that when the darkness of error has been expelled, they may be guided to faith; but children through their parents that the parents may know what they ought to teach them lest the sacrament of baptism be impeded by a human defect, although it attain its end.

CHAPTER EIGHT

THE INTEGRITY OF CONFIRMATION

1. As to the sacrament of confirmation, we must hold that a vocal form is required for its integrity. According to the more common practice it is: I sign thee with the sign of the cross and confirm thee with the chrism of salvation in the name of the Father and of the Son and of the Holy Ghost. Amen. Chrism is also required, and this is made up of olive oil and of balsam. When the sign of the cross is marked with chrism on the forehead by the hand of the bishop with the afore-named arrangement of the words of confirmation, the sacrament is received and man is strengthened by it so that as a fighter he must boldly and publicly acknowledge the name of Christ.

2. The explanation of this is as follows: Just as our restorative principle, namely, the incarnate Word, was conceived from eternity in the heart of the Father and in time appeared to man in flesh, so He restores no one unless he receives Him with a believing heart and evinces his belief by external manifestation in the form of a suitable profession. Such is a profession confessing the whole truth, not only the speculative but also the practical. This is the case where there is not only the "identity of intellect, speech, and the thing," [18] but where the whole man is conformed to truth according to the understanding of reason, according to the agreement of the will,

[18] Aristotle, *De praedicamentis.*

and the adherence to virtue so that the confession is from the whole heart, whole soul, and whole mind, from a pure heart, a good conscience, and an unfeigned faith. Such a profession is complete, clear, and undaunted, so that it is a complete whole by reason of the being from whom it comes, clear by reason of the being in whose presence it is made, and undaunted by reason of the being by whom that profession has to be made. Because a tender-minded man is not well suited to do this unless he is first strengthened by the hand of grace from above, the sacrament of confirmation has been divinely instituted as immediately following baptism.

3. Because "an end imposes the necessity for those things which tend to the end," [19] this sacrament ought to be completed as required by the aforenamed profession and by its conditions, namely, the three aforenamed. First, because this profession should be complete, and there is no completeness of profession unless one confesses Christ to be true man, crucified for man, and the same true incarnate Son of God coequal in all things in the Trinity with the Father and the Holy Ghost, hence in the vocal form expression is given not only of the act of confirmation but also of the sign of the cross and the name of the most blessed Trinity.

4. Furthermore, because the profession ought to be clear by reason of the being in whose presence it is made, and it has to be made in the presence of God and men and it cannot please God unless the light of intelligence and the splendor of conscience are present, nor can it please our neighbor unless the fragrance of good reputation and honest life are present, hence to designate these by an external symbol, transparent oil of olives and the fragrant oil of balsam are mixed so that the mixture signifies that the profession for which this sacrament disposes one ought to possess united clarity of conscience and of undertaking together with the sweet odor of life and reputation, lest there be some contradiction between language

[19] *Ibid., Physics*, II, 9.

and conscience or between language and reputation which would cause such a profession to be rejected by man and disapproved by Christ.

5. Lastly, because such a profession ought to be undaunted so that a person does not out of shame or fear refuse to tell the truth, and so that he is not in time of persecution afraid or ashamed publicly to confess the ignominious death of Christ on the cross for fear of suffering a similar punishment and ignominious passion and such a fear and shame appear especially on the face and principally on the forehead, hence, to ward off all shamefacedness and fear, the powerful hand which confirms is there imposed and the cross is marked on the forehead so that one may not be ashamed publicly to profess that death or fear to sustain any punishment or ignominy whatsoever for the profession of the name of Christ, if the occasion should so demand. Then a person shall be, as it were, a true fighter anointed for battle; a strong soldier bearing the symbol of his King on his forehead and the triumphal standard of His cross with which he is prepared to penetrate the mighty strongholds of the enemy. One cannot be free to proclaim the glory of the cross if the punishment and ignominy of the cross is feared. Thus St. Andrew says: "If I were ashamed of the ignominy of the cross, I would not proclaim the glory of the cross." [20]

CHAPTER NINE

THE INTEGRITY OF THE EUCHARIST

1. As to the sacrament of the Eucharist, this must be held: that in this sacrament not only is the true body and blood of Christ signified but it is actually contained under the double

---

[20] "Passion of St. Andrew" in Surius, *Historia seu vitae sanctorum*, XI, 743, § 4; Gallandi, *Bibliotheca*, I, 155.

species, namely, bread and wine, in one and not a twofold sacrament. This occurs after the consecration by the priest which is completed by saying over the bread the vocal form instituted by our Lord: This is My body; and over the wine: This is the chalice of My blood. When these words are spoken by a priest with the proper intention, each element is transubstantiated in substance into the body and blood of Jesus Christ even though the sensible species remain. The entire Christ is wholly contained in each of them, not in a circumscribed manner, but sacramentally. These words also show us that anyone worthily receiving the bread, not only sacramentally but through faith and charity by spiritual digestion becomes more a part of the mystical body of Christ and is in himself remade and cleansed. But he who approaches unworthily eats and drinks his own judgment, not discerning the most holy body of Christ.[21]

2. The explanation of this is as follows: Because our restorative principle, namely, the incarnate Word, is most sufficient in power and most wise in matters of sense, He gave us sacraments according to what His wisdom and sufficiency require. Because He is most sufficient, in bestowing remedies for sickness and gifts of grace, He not only instituted a sacrament which would generate us in the being of grace, as baptism, and one which would increase and strengthen those already generated, as confirmation, but also a sacrament which would nourish those generated and increased, as the sacrament of the Eucharist. Hence these three sacraments are given to all who embrace the faith. Because our nourishment from the point of view of the being of grace is accompanied in each of the faithful by preservation of devotion to God, love for our neighbor, and delight within himself, and devotion to God is accomplished through the offering of sacrifice, and love toward our neighbor through mutual participation in one sacrament, and delight within oneself through the refreshment of the

[21] I Cor. 11:29.

nourishment, our restorative principle has given us the sacrament of the Eucharist as the sacrifice of an offering, the sacrament of communion, and the viaticum of refreshment.

3. Because our restorative principle is not only most sufficient but most wise, and it is His nature to do all things orderly, He so ordered and arranged things that we would have a sacrifice, a sacrament, and a nourishment which He conformed to the time of revealed grace, to the state of the way, and to our capacity. First, since the time of revealed grace requires that no oblation be offered except a pure, placating, and complete one, and there is no such offering except the one offered on the cross, namely, the body and blood of Christ, it is necessary that the body of Christ be contained in this sacrament not only figuratively but truly as an oblation proper to this time. Similarly, because in the time of grace it is proper that the sacrament of communion and love should not only signify communion and love but also stimulate them so that "it brings about what it represents," [22] and it is proper that it should especially rouse us to mutual love and unite the members to the highest degree and be the unity of the head from which mutual love flows into us through the diffuse, uniting, and transformative strength of love, hence the true body and immaculate flesh of Christ are contained in this sacrament so that, diffusing Himself in us and uniting us to one another and transforming us into Himself through most ardent love by which He gave Himself to us, He offered Himself in our behalf and gave Himself up for us and exists with us to the end of the world. Thus the restoration suitable for the state of grace is a spiritual, universal, and salutary restoration. Spiritual restoration is the word of life.[23] Hence the spiritual restoration of the spirit in the flesh is the incarnate Word or the flesh of the Word which is the common and salutary bread because, although it is one, yet all are saved through it. Because no other spiritual, universal, and salutary bread could

---

[22] Peter Lombard, op. cit., IV, 4, 3.
[23] Cf. John 6:69.

be given other than the true body of Christ Himself, it must be truly contained in this sacrament which requires the perfection of a placating sacrifice, a uniting sacrament, and a restorative nourishment: and these matters ought to happen in the time of the New Testament, of revealed grace, and of the truth of Christ.

4. Again, because in the wayfaring state it is not fit that we see Christ openly on account of the veil of obscurity and the merit of faith and it is not fit that we touch the flesh of Christ with our teeth because of the horror of such unseemly crudeness and the immortality of Christ's body, the body and blood of Christ must be veiled in sacred symbols and in fitting and expressive similitudes. And because nothing is more fitting for our restoration than the food of bread and the drink of wine, nothing is likewise more fitting to signify the unity of the true and mystical body of Christ than bread made from the most pure grain and wine pressed from pure grapes taken together, hence this sacrament ought to be represented under these species rather than any others. And because Christ ought to be present under these species not through a change made in Him but rather through a change made in them, it follows that, at the utterance of the two above-mentioned expressions which point out the existence of Christ under these species, there is a change of each substance into His body and blood, and the accidents alone remain as signs denoting and expressing His body.

5. Because the blessed and glorious body of Christ cannot be divided into its parts and cannot be separated from the soul or from the highest divinity, hence under each species there is the one, entire, and indivisible Christ, namely, body, soul, and God. Hence in each is the one and most simple sacrament containing the entire Christ. And because every part of the species signifies the body of Christ, the whole body so exists in the whole species and it is in any part of it, whether it be undivided or separated. Hence the body is not there as circumscribed, as occupying space, as having position, as per-

ceptible through any corporeal and human sense, but it is hidden from all sense so that faith may have its place and merit. That we may not perceive Him directly, these accidents, although they exist without their subject, have every function which they had previously as long as they contain within themselves the body of Christ and this is as long as they exist with their natural properties and are fit for eating.

6. Lastly, because our capacity for receiving Christ effectively lies not in our flesh but in our spirit, not in our stomach but in our mind, and because our mind does not come in contact with Christ except through knowledge and love, through faith and charity such that faith illumines for understanding and love inflames for devotion, therefore if anyone is to approach the sacrament worthily he ought to partake spiritually so that he may thus eat through the knowledge of faith and receive through the devotion of love. Hence the recipient does not transform Christ into himself but rather is himself translated into Christ's mystical body. For this reason it is quite evident that he who receives in a lukewarm manner, without devotion and inconsiderately, eats and drinks judgment unto himself, because he brings dishonor to such a great sacrament. So it is recommended that those who judge themselves less pure of mind or body or even without devotion, postpone reception until they are prepared for the eating of the true Lamb and may approach in a pure, devout, and circumspect manner.[24]

7. Hence this sacrament was ordered to be received with as much solemnity in place, time, words, prayers, and vestments as in the case of the celebration of Mass so that the celebrating priests as well as the recipients would receive the gift of grace through which they are cleansed, stimulated, perfected, restored, vivified, and most ardently borne up into Christ Himself through embracing love.

[24] The present teaching on the reception of Holy Communion requires only (1) that the communicant be in the state of grace, (2) that he be fasting, and (3) that he have the right intention, that is, not merely from habit, not out of vanity, and not for some worldly human advantage, but to please God.

CHAPTER TEN

THE INTEGRITY OF PENANCE

1. As to the sacrament of penance, this must be held: that it is "the second plank after the shipwreck" [25] by which he who has been wrecked through mortal sin can return as long as he is in the present life, when and as often as he wishes to invoke divine mercy. The integral parts of this sacrament are: contrition in the soul, oral confession, and actual satisfaction. Out of these penance is integrated when the sinner, after having perpetrated mortal sin, deserts the same by deed, accuses himself by word, and detests his sin within his soul, proposing never to repeat the sin. After these things have been done in the required manner together with absolution given by one with orders, the key, and the jurisdiction, man is absolved from sin, reunited with the Church, and reconciled with Christ through the medium of the priestly key. The priest must have in his power not only absolution but also the power of excommunication and its remission which he appropriately has to obtain from the bishop as the spouse of the Church.

2. The explanation of this is as follows: Because our restorative principle, namely, the incarnate Word, in so far as He is the Word, is the fountain of truth and wisdom, and in so far as He is incarnate, is the fountain of piety and indulgence, hence He ought to restore the human race through the remedies of sacraments and especially by attacking the greatest sickness, which is mortal sin, according to what is befitting for a pious priest, an experienced physician, and a just judge, so that in our cure the highest mercy, highest prudence, and highest justice of the incarnate Word may appear.

3. First, because in our cure from mortal sin through penance the highest mercy of the most pious Priest, Christ Him-

[25] Jerome, *Epistle* 130 (alias 8), 9.

self, must be present, and the highest mercy of the Priest surpasses all human sins, no matter what or how numerous the
kind or how often they have been committed, hence sinners
receive the pardon of the most clement Priest Himself, not
once or twice but as often as they suppliantly invoke the mercy
of God. And because divine mercy is then truly and suppliantly invoked when man possesses the lamentation of penance
and because man can turn to penance as long as he is in the
present life, for he is capable of turning to both good and
evil, it follows that every sinner no matter how great, varied,
or frequent his sin can have refuge in the sacrament of penance through which he receives remission of his sins.

4. Again, because in our cure the highest prudence of the
most experienced physician, Christ Himself, ought to be manifested, and the prudence of a physician lies in applying contrary remedies not only to remove sickness but to cut off its
cause, and since one sins against God with delight, consent,
and perpetration, namely, in heart, mouth, and deed, hence
the most prudent physician has so instituted things that
against the disorderliness of the sinner and his concealed
delight in these three powers, namely, the effective, interpre-
tative, and operative, there should be set the reformation of
the sinner in the same three powers through the penance of
sorrow conceived in the heart, through compunction, expressed orally through confession and consummated in deed
by satisfaction. And because all mortal sins turn men away
from the one God and are opposed to the one grace and per-
vert the one principal righteousness of man, hence, that the
remedy of penance may be sufficiently integrated from its own
parts, man must have repentance for all sins: for the past
through displeasure for the perpetrated acts, for the present
through cessation from perpetrating the acts, and for the future through the resolve of never falling back into the same
or into any other kind of sin so that thus, by his totally
withdrawing from sin through penance, divine grace is

received and through it pardon is obtained for all his sins.

5. Lastly, because in our cure the righteous justice of the judge, Christ Himself, ought to be manifested, and because it is not for Him to judge in His own person until the last and final judgment, He ought to provide judges for particular judgments before the end. And because such judges are like mediators between offended God and offending man, close to Christ and preferred by the people, and those who are particularly close to and intimate with the Lord by reason of their office are those who are particularly consecrated to His ministry, namely, the priests, hence to all established in the sacerdotal order and to them alone the twofold power of the key is given, namely, the key of knowledge for discriminating, and the key which is the power of binding and loosing, for adjudicating and for dispensing the benefit of absolution.

6. Because in order to avoid confusion not everyone who desires it is given preference in the militant Church, since the ecclesiastical hierarchy itself ought to be ordained in conformity with judicial power, the power of binding and loosing was granted first to the one, first, and highest priest, to whom universal power was granted as the highest head, then this power was divided according to the particular Churches so that it descends from the one head first to the bishops and then to the priests. Hence, though every priest has orders and the key, the use of the key extends only to those who are ordinarily subject to them, unless it is given to a priest by one who has ordinary jurisdiction. Since that jurisdiction is chiefly in the highest head and then in a bishop and lastly in a priest having the care of souls, it can be given by any one of these to another, sufficiently indeed by the lowest one, more by the middle one, and most by the highest one.[26]

7. And because jurisdiction rests in the supreme pontiff and also in the bishops not only for judging between God

[26] The faculties of confession can be given by the pope and the bishop, but not by a priest to another.

and man in secrecy, but also for judging between man and man in the open: for example, judging those intrusted with the government and custody of the Church, for they are like a wife given to her husband; hence the prelates have the sword, which they can use to strike for the defense of justice in excommunication, and the power of giving in abundance from the treasures of the merits of the Church which they have intrusted to them by the head and the members, and this power is remission, so that as judges of the true God they possess the whole power of binding and loosing by which they may strike the impenitent, repress the rebels, and absolve and reconcile those truly penitent to God and holy mother Church.

CHAPTER ELEVEN

THE INTEGRITY OF EXTREME UNCTION

1. As to the sacrament of extreme unction, this must be held: that it is the sacrament of those departing from this life, preparing and disposing them for perfect health; it is also effective in expunging venial sins and for the recovery of health if this is for the good of the infirm person. For the integrity of this sacrament, simple but consecrated oil is required, as are the recitation of prayers and the anointing of seven designated parts of the one who is sick, namely, the eyes, ears, nostrils, lips, hands, feet, and loins.[27] This sacrament should be given only to adults who desire it, who are imminently in danger of death, and then only by the administration of a priest. From this it is evident that there is a sevenfold difference between this sacrament and confirmation, namely, in effect, matter, form, recipient, minister, place, and time.

2. The explanation of this is as follows: Because our restorative principle, namely, the incarnate Word, restores us in so far as He is the mediator of God and men, the man Jesus Christ, and in so far as He is Jesus, has to save us and, in so

---

[27] The loins are no longer anointed.

far as He is Christ the anointed has to allow anointing grace to flow into others, hence He must bestow salutary anointing on His own members in His sacraments. Because the soul, to be perfectly healthy, requires a triple kind of health, namely, for the strain of action, for the sweetness of contemplation, and for the happiness of comprehension, and the first is for those entering the ranks of the Church, the second is for those directing the ranks, whose duty it is to teach others, and the third is for those departing from the ranks through death, hence the Lord begins the sacramental anointing in confirmation and gives the middle anointing in the pontifical order and the last anointing when we are imminently in danger of death.

3. Because "the end imposes the necessity of those things which tend to the end," [28] this sacrament ought to be performed and also integrated, received and dispensed, for this end. The first, because the performance of this sacrament ought to be governed by the end. There is an end because this sacrament was introduced to secure and expedite our salvation and perpetual happiness. This is brought about through devotion which raises us up and through remission of venial sins and other consequences which press us downwards. Hence this sacrament possesses efficacy in arousing devotion, in remitting venial sins, and in more easily cleansing the blot of sin. Because it aids many sick persons to live in order to accumulate merits, the sacrament by making the soul vigorous in good and by unburdening it of evil, also frequently alleviates sickness. Thus it is that St. James says that "the prayer of faith shall save the sick man . . . and if he be in sins, they shall be forgiven him" (Jas. 5:15).

4. Again, because the institution of this sacrament ought to meet the requirement of its end, and this is the acquisition of spiritual salvation through the remission of sins, and such salvation means health and cleanness of the conscience within us by which the heavenly Judge judges, there ought to be sim-

[28] Aristotle, *Physics*, II, 9.

ple and consecrated oil in this sacrament because such oil denotes sanctity and splendor in the conscience within us. Because mortal man does not have power over that salvation, we use prayer and vocal form with humble words to procure the gift of grace. And because the soul is the center of the spiritual infirmities in the body which spring from the four principal powers of our body, namely, the sensitive, interpretive, generative, and progressive, the members appropriate to these powers must be anointed. Because there are five members appropriate to the five senses, namely, the eyes for seeing, the ears for hearing, the nose for smelling, the hands for feeling, and the mouth for tasting and also for another power, namely, speaking (the interpretive), and also the feet serve for walking (the progressive), and the loins for generation—and it is unsuitable and shameful to touch or even to mention by name the generating organs—hence the anointing ought to be in the seven above-mentioned places so that thus man is guided through this sacrament to complete health through the cleansing of every venial sin.

5. Lastly, because the reception of that sacrament depends on its purpose, and the purpose is a more rapid journey to heaven through the unburdening of venial sin and the turning of the mind to God, it ought not to be given except to adults who have sinned venially, and to none except petitioners elevated by devotion, and only to those in danger and, as it were, in a passage to another status. And because this is the sacrament of those in danger, and yet has sacred matter, namely, consecrated oil, it ought to be commonly distributed by priests because of the chance of its omission and because consecrated oil must not be handled except by consecrated hands.[29]

---

[29] Additional limitations exist today. Extreme unction may not be repeated in the same sickness unless the sick person, after receiving extreme unction, has recovered and has fallen again into the danger of death. This sacrament is given conditionally if there is doubt whether the sick person has attained the use of reason, whether he is in danger of death, or whether he is already dead. Cf. CIC, can. 940 f.

6. From the differences in the ends of confirmation and extreme unction arise the differences in efficacy, in matter and form, in time and place, in recipient and minister: in efficacy because the former sacrament disposes one to contend better, the latter for leaving this world more quickly; in matter because the former uses oil mixed with balsam, the latter pure oil; in form because the former is indicative, but the latter deprecative; in place because the former is on the forehead, the latter on many members; in time because the former occurs in health, the latter in sickness; in the recipient because the former is for adults and children, the latter only for adults; in the minister because the former is given by bishops, the latter by any priest whatsoever. All these differences derive from the end because, as has become clear, a difference in the proximate ends introduces a difference in the means ultimately designed for those ends.

CHAPTER TWELVE

THE INTEGRITY OF ORDERS

1. As to the sacrament of orders, we must hold that "orders is a certain sign by which spiritual power is given through ordination." [30] Though orders is one of the seven sacraments, there are seven steps to orders. The first is porter, the second reader, the third exorcist, the fourth acolyte, the fifth subdeacon, the sixth deacon, and the seventh priest. Under these, by way of preparation, are the clerical tonsure and the reader of the psalms and conversely, the bishop, patriarch, and pope are above them as a complement because orders flow from them and ought to be dispensed with proper signs for sight and hearing, to preserve the required solemnity in place, time, office, and person.

[30] Peter Lombard, *op. cit.*, IV, 24, 13.

2. The explanation of this is as follows: Because for our salvation the restorative principle, namely, the incarnate Word, as God and man, has instituted the remedies of the sacraments ordinately, distinctly, and powerfully to accord with the dictates of His goodness, wisdom, and power, He entrusted to men the remedies of the sacraments to be dispensed not in any way but in the way which order, discretion, and power dictate. Some persons ought to be distinguished and separated to carry out this office, and this power should be given to them by a proper law. Because a differentiation of this kind ought not to be made except through sacred signs and the sacraments are such, there ought to be some sacrament which is a sacred sign, ordinate, distinctive, and potent, for the dispensation of the other sacraments in a distinctiive, potent, and ordinate manner. Therefore orders is defined as "a certain sign in which spiritual power is given by ordination" so that at the same time the three above-named qualities are present in its description and from these we can in summation say what things are required for the integrity of orders.

3. First, therefore, because orders is a distinctive sign and hidden from all people so that one ordained is completely set aside for the service of God, a certain distinction precedes orders in the tonsure and crown. It indicates the cutting off of temporal appetites and the elevation of the mind to eternity so that every cleric is shown to be destined for the service of God. Therefore one says in receiving the crown: "The Lord is the portion of my inheritance," etc.[31] And because such a one ought to be instructed in the divine praises which are found principally in the psalms, the position of reader of the psalms [32] also ought to precede orders as a preamble which Isidore in a broader sense enumerates among the orders.[33]

4. Secondly, because orders is an ordinating sign and also

---

[31] Ps. 15:5.
[32] This office is now obsolete.
[33] Isidore of Seville, Etymologia, VII, 12, 13; De officiis ecclesiasticis, 12; Epistola ad Ludifredum.

ordinate in itself, and orders consists in a complete separation and distinction of grades consistent with the requirements of a sevenfold grace for whose dispensation the sacrament of orders is mainly designed, there are seven orders leading by degrees to the priesthood, which is the culmination of orders because it is the office of the priest to consecrate the sacrament of the body of Christ in whom there is a fullness of all grace. Hence the other six are subministrative and, as it were, steps through which one is raised to the throne of Solomon.[34] Thus the preliminary orders are six because of the perfection of that number, for six is the first perfect number, and the perfection and sufficiency of the office of the ministry require such a number. It is fitting that some with orders administer as if from a more remote place, some as if from a nearer place, and some as if from the nearest place so that nothing may be lacking in an orderly ministry. Because each of these orders increases in the amount of cleansing and illumination, there are six ministerial orders, and the seventh is the most perfect of all for to it is intrusted the sacrament of the altar, which is delegated to one order as the final and complete end.

5. Lastly, because orders is a potent sign not only with respect to the dispensation of the other sacraments but also with respect to itself, and power over power is excellent power, hence orders should have not only simple power, and power of this kind is simple orders, but it should also have the perfection of power, and power of this kind exists in those who can properly confer orders. And because excellence is diluted as it descends and is unified as it ascends, there are many bishops, fewer archbishops, very few patriarchs, and one father of fathers who is rightly called pope, the one, first and greatest spiritual father of all fathers, and on the other hand of all the faithful, the distinguished hierarch, the single spouse, undivided head, highest pontiff, vicar of Christ, fountain, origin, and ruler of all ecclesiastical principalities. From him, the

[34] III Kings 10:18 f.

highest of all, ordained power is derived even down to the lowest members of the Church as the great dignity in the ecclesiastical hierarchy requires.

6. And because this dignity rests principally in orders, the sacrament ought not to be dispensed except with great discretion and solemnity, and accordingly neither by everyone nor to everyone nor in every place nor at an indiscriminate time, but rather to literate persons, honorable, and free from all unsuitable irregularities, to one fasting, in a sacred place, during Mass, and at times set by ecclesiastical order, and then by bishops to whom, because of their excellence, are reserved the following: the dispensation of orders, confirmation by the imposition of hands, consecration of monks and abbots, and the dedication of churches. Because of their solemnity, all these ought not to be administered except by those who have preeminent power.

CHAPTER THIRTEEN

THE INTEGRITY OF MATRIMONY

1. As to the sacrament of matrimony, this must be held in summation: that "matrimony is the legitimate union of a man and a woman retaining their individual manner of life." [35] This union existed not only after sin but before sin. Formerly the sacrament of matrimony was instituted as an office, now it is not only an office but also a remedy against the sickness of concupiscence. Formerly it signified the union of God and the soul, now besides this it signifies the union of Christ and the Church and of the two natures in a unity of person. This union is created through the free consent of each person outwardly expressed in some sensible sign, but it has to be consummated through carnal union. Matrimony is

[35] Justinian, *Instituta*, I, 9.

begun by words of promise, ratified by present words, but consummated in carnal union. This sacrament has three benefits, namely, "faith, offspring, and a sacrament," [36] and it has twelve [37] impediments which hamper those uniting and separate those already united as is shown in these verses: [38]

Error, disparity in circumstance, vow, blood relationship, crime,
Disparity in religion, force, orders, existing marital ties, spiritual affinity,
If you are affianced, if perchance you shall not be able to be together;
These things prevent marriage from being entered into and break up unions already entered into.

2. The explanation of this is as follows: Because our restorative principle, namely, the incarnate Word, in so far as He is the Word of God, is the fountain of the highest wisdom and in so far as He is incarnate is the fountain of mercy on earth, therefore in so far as He is the uncreated Word, He is, because of His highest wisdom, the formative principle of the human race, and in so far as He is incarnate, is the reformative principle of it out of His highest mercy. Therefore He restores the human race through His mercy because formerly, because of His wisdom, He made it restorable, which quality His supreme order required because He made the human race able to stand, able to fall, and able to be restored, as was shown in preceding chapters.[39] Because the Word of God in His wisdom made man, as was fitting, able to stand, able to fall, and able to rise. He ordained the human race to be propa-

36 Augustine, *De Genesi ad litteram*, IX, 7, 42.

37 Quarrachi editors state that Bonaventure includes age, in the second, disparity in circumstance. But as is seen later in this chapter, this verse includes in spiritual affinity (*honestas*) what Bonaventure calls two: spiritual affinity (*affinitas*) and reflection on public decency (*publicae justitiae honestas*).

38 Error, conditio, votum, cognatio, crimen, Cultus disparitas, vis, ordo, ligamen, honestas; Si sis affines, si forte coire nequibis; Haec sociana vetant coniugia, iuncta retractant.

39 Cf. *supra*, Part I, chap. 1; Part II, chap. 9; Part III, chap. 1.

gated in such a manner as would by its very nature be congruous with its power to stand and to be cured, just as there is
in that propagation something of sin, namely, concupiscence,
which brings about sickness. And because man's original state
derived from the union of the soul itself to God and through
a unitive love in a most chaste, singular, and individual way,
and because the remedy came about from the union of a divine and human nature in the unity of a hypostasis and person, a unity, I say, introduced by divine grace as single and
individual, hence God has instituted from the beginning that
propagation should come about through the individual and
single union of man and woman which before the time of sin
signified the union of God and the soul or of God and the
subcelestial hierarchy but after sin the union of God and
human nature, or of Christ and the Church. Thus it is a sacrament before and after man's fall, though first in one way and
then in another as regards its signification and use. Since marriage was a sacrament before sickness came, concupiscence
which came through sin has to be excused through matrimony
rather than avail to corrupt it. This is so because sickness does
not corrupt the remedy, but the remedy has to cure the sickness. From this it appears what matrimony is and in what way
it was divinely introduced.

3. Again, because any of the above-named spiritual unions
signified in the sacrament of matrimony is a union of one who
is the active and influencing party and the other who is the
passive and receiving party, and this occurs through a bond of
love which proceeds from nothing but the will, hence matrimony ought to be the union of two persons, different in activity and passivity, namely, the male and the female sex, and
this union must follow the untrammeled consent of the will.
And because the will does not appear outwardly except
through a sign expressing it, mutual consent must be expressed outwardly. But because consent as a promise is not
consent itself but a promise of consent, and consent before

the union does not make a complete union because the parties are not as yet one flesh, matrimony is said to be begun through words of promise, confirmed through present words, but completed in carnal union because the parties are one flesh and become one body. Hence marriage completely signifies that union which exists between us and Christ. Then the body of one is given over completely to the body of the other according to the power of one's partner to procreate.

4. There are three benefits of matrimony, namely, a sacrament because of its insoluble bond, faith because of the discharge of what is due, and offspring, an effect following upon both.

5. Lastly, because the above-stated matrimonial union ought to proceed from free consent to the union of different persons under one law of matrimony, and this can be hampered in twelve ways, there are twelve impediments of matrimony. There are required for matrimonial consent: freedom in consent, freedom on the part of the consenter, and fitness for union. Freedom in consent is destroyed in two ways by two kinds of involition, namely, through error and through force. Thus these are the first two impediments, namely, error and force. Freedom on the part of the consenter is destroyed through his being bound to another, either to God or to man. If to God, either through an expressed vow or through something which has a vow attached to it. The first is in a vow, the second in orders. If one is bound to man, there are two bonds: either in existing or preceding ties: the first is the bond by which one is bound to his wife, the second is in crime when an adulterer or an adulteress has brought about the death of the consort, or, if he is still living, has given a promise of marriage. Thus there are four impediments, namely, vow, orders, ties, and crime. Fitness for union requires a suitable distance between persons, and this is destroyed through too close relationship or too great a disparity. Too close relationship comes through blood relationship or

through something similar to blood relationship, as legal and spiritual relation: either it comes through mingling of the sexes or through the relationship of sponsors. Thus there are three impediments, namely, blood relationship, spiritual affinity, and reflection on public decency. Too great a disparity exists either in regard to defects which are natural, as when the parties cannot be joined bodily, or in regard to fortuitous defects which are not in our dispensation, as when one is a slave and the other is free, or in regard to differences in the matter of religion, as when one is baptized but the other is not. Thus there are three impediments: incapability of union, disparity of condition, and disparity of religion. Hence twelve impediments in all, as the Holy Ghost teaches, are recognized by the Church, to whom the sacrament of marriage in particular is intrusted, although all the sacraments are so intrusted, for regulation of the various situations which can arise and because of the sickness attached to it. This sickness is especially infectious and does not at all tend toward moderation. Therefore it is for the Church to limit the degrees of blood relationship, just as she sees necessary at the time and to adjudge persons legitimately or illegitimately married and to decree separation. But the Church ought never nor can it annul a marriage which has been legitimately entered into, because whom God has joined, no one, howsoever great his power, can separate, since the jurisdiction of judging the universe remains in God Himself.

PART SEVEN

THE FINAL JUDGMENT

CHAPTER ONE

THE JUDGMENT IN GENERAL

1. After a brief discussion of the Trinity of God, the creation of the world, the corruption of sin, the incarnation of the Word, the grace of the Holy Ghost, and the sacramental remedy, we now undertake in the seventh and last part a brief treatment of the final judgment. On this point we must hold these truths in summa: that there will undoubtedly be a future judgment of everyone in the universe, and in this judgment God the Father through our Lord Jesus Christ will judge the living and the dead, the good and the wicked, rendering to each according to his works.[1] In this judgment there will be an opening of the books, namely, of the consciences of men through which the merits and demerits of everyone in the universe will be made known to himself and to others, and this by the power of that book of life, namely, of the incarnate Word. He will not be seen in the divine form except by the good and He will be seen in the human form in which He will disclose His verdict alike to the good and to the wicked, though He will appear in the same form as terrible to the wicked and attractive to the just.

2. The explanation of this is as follows: Since the first principle, by the very fact that it is first, exists from itself, according to itself, and because of itself, it is by this very fact the efficient cause, the form, and the end, producing, ruling, and perfecting the universe in such a way that, as it produces according to the height of its power, it also rules as the rectitude of truth requires and consummates matters as the fullness of

[1] Matt. 16:27; 25:31 ff.

its goodness requires. Because the height of the highest power requires that there be the production of a creature in image as well as one in vestige, of a rational creature as well as an irrational, not only of a creature moved by natural force but of one moved by a free will, and because a creature which is in image, since it is capable of attaining God, is capable of beatitude, and a rational creature is capable of learning, and a creature having freedom of will is capable of following the law of justice or opposing it, hence the rectitude of truth ought to have imposed a law on man in which it invites him to beatitude, instructs him in truth, and binds him to justice, but in such a way that it does not coerce the freedom of the will into being unable to relinquish justice for the desire of its own will or to follow justice. It follows such a path since "it so directs the things which it has created that it permits their own motives to guide them." [2] Because fullness of goodness in consummating matters develops according as the height of power and the rectitude of truth require, hence the consummation of beatitude is not granted by the highest goodness except to those who have observed the justice which was imposed by the rectitude of truth and who have accepted discipline and who have loved that highest and eternal blessedness more than transitory goods. And because some have done this and others have done the opposite on account of the diversity of desires which lie hidden within us and in the state of the wayfarer concur with each one's will, hence a universal judgment must follow to manifest the height of virtue, the rectitude of truth, and the fullness of goodness. At that judgment there will be a just distribution of rewards, an open declaration of merits, and an irrevocable rendering of sentences so that in the just distribution of what is due there may appear the fullness of the highest goodness, in the open declaration of merits there may appear the rectitude of truth, and in the irrevocable rendering of sentences there may appear the height of the highest

2 Augustine, *De civitate Dei*, VII, 30.

virtue and power. The first is so because a just distribution shows the faults for which punishment is due or it shows justice for which glory is due, and all the sons of Adam have either one or the other coming. Hence all must be judged by a judgment of retribution so that the just may be glorified and the wicked condemned.

3. Again, because the open declaration of merits requires that there should simultaneously appear what ought to be done and what was done or omitted by the freedom of the human will according to the variety of consciences, the books of consciences will be opened to disclose their merits and the book of life to disclose that justice according to which men's merits ought to be approved or disapproved. And because the book of life is a book in which all things are written simultaneously and most clearly and they are truthfully written in our consciences, hence from the concurrence of the opening of these books there shall come an open declaration of all merits so that the secrets of every heart shall be made known to itself and to others. Whence, as Augustine holds, that book is "a force from which all things are wonderfully recalled to every one's memory," [3] so that the equity of the divine judgments may clearly show itself in the brightest light of truth.

4. Finally, because the irrevocable rendering of sentences ought to be made by one who can be heard and seen and by one who can announce it and the greatest light cannot be seen by all because darkened eyes cannot see it owing to the fact that we cannot see Him face to face without a godlikeness of mind and joy of heart, the judge must appear in the form of a creature. Because a pure creature does not have the greatest authority, and judgment cannot be announced without such, our judge must be both God so that He judges by the greatest authority, and man so that He may be seen by and communicate with sinners in human form. Because the same voice of decision terrifies the guilty and assures

[3] *Ibid.*, XX, 14.

the innocent, His one form will gladden the just and conversely terrify the guilty.

CHAPTER TWO

THE ANTECEDENTS OF THE JUDGMENT: THE PUNISHMENT OF PURGATORY

1. We ought to consider in particular certain antecedents of the final judgment. There are two antecedents, namely, the punishment of purgatory and the ecclesiastical intercessions.

2. First we must hold these truths about the punishment of purgatory: that the fire of purgatory is a corporeal fire which punishes the souls of the just who have not in this life completed their punishment and the satisfaction for sin. Some are punished more and some less according as they departed this life with more or less imperfection. The souls in purgatory are punished less severely than those in hell but more severely than those in this world. But their punishment is not so severe as to prevent hope and their knowledge that they are not in hell. However, they do not advert to this fact very often because of the magnitude of their punishments. With the infliction of the punishment of corporeal fire, their souls are purged from guilt and dregs and also from the remainders of sins. When they are sufficiently purged, they immediately depart and enter into the glory of paradise.

3. The explanation of this is as follows: Since the first principle, by the very fact that it is first, is best and most perfect and, by the very fact that it is best, is most amorous of good and most hateful of evil, the greatest goodness does not permit good to go unrewarded nor ought it to permit evil to go unpunished. Because just men sometimes die without having wholly satisfied their punishment in this life, and because the merit of eternal life cannot go undeservedly to them and

the blemish of sin cannot go unpunished lest the beauty of universal order be disturbed, it is necessary that they be finally rewarded and that they be temporarily punished according to their deserts and the guilt of their sins. Because a sin that was committed was an offense against the divine majesty, an injury to the Church, and a deforming of the divine image impressed on our soul, especially if it be a mortal sin, though even a venial sin operates in this way, and because that offense requires a punishment, and that injury requires a satisfaction, and that deformation requires a purging, it is necessary that that punishment be justly punitive, suitable in satisfaction, and sufficiently purgative.

4. First, because that punishment ought to be justly punitive and because the spirit which by contempt for the eternal and highest good threw itself down to the depths ought justly to be subjected to the lower spirits so that it may receive punishment by those who caused it to fall into sin and through whom it hated God and made itself detestable, hence the order of divine justice demands that the spirit should be punished by a material fire so that, just as the soul is united to the body in the order of nature to give it life, so it should be united to the body in the material fire according to the order of justice so that the thing punishable is united to the punishing element from which it receives its punishment. Because just men who are in the state of grace are deserving only of temporary punishment and are deserving of greater punishment in proportion as they have committed greater sins and done less penance, they are punished by the material fire temporarily, some longer, others shorter, some more severely, others less, according as the guilt of their offense demands. The illustrious doctor Augustine says: "Necessarily in proportion as sorrow burns, love remains." [4] The greater the difficulty in purging anyone, the more in the depth of his heart there has adhered an intimate love of things mundane.

[4] *Ibid.*, XXVI, 4.

5. Further, because the punishment of purgatory ought to be in satisfaction, and satisfaction requires a freedom of will and the status of the wayfarer, and most certainly because there does not then exist a state of merit and such punishments certainly do not reflect the idea of being voluntary, it follows necessarily that what is lacking on the part of freedom in the will in so accepting is to be made up for by the severity of the punishment. Because those who are purged possess grace which they can no longer dissipate, they cannot be enshrouded by an inner sadness nor can they fall into despair or blasphemy, nor do they wish to fly forth somewhere. Hence, though they are punished severely, yet the length and severity of the punishment are less than in hell, and they undoubtedly realize their state is unlike that of those who are tortured in hell without thereby remedying the situation.

6. Finally, because that punishment ought to be purgative and that purging is spiritual, either that fire necessarily has a spiritual power given it by God or, as I believe more strongly, the power of grace residing within each, aided by an external punishment, sufficiently purges that soul punished for its offenses and freed from the weight of its sins so that there remains no unfitness for glory. Because such spirits are at last disposed to receive the godlikeness of glory and because the gates are opened and the purging complete, those spirits in whom the fire of love reaches upwards and no basis is present for detention on account of impurity of the soul or of fault, necessarily fly to heaven. It is not fitting that divine mercy or justice should further defer glory when it finds the recipient suitable. It would be a great punishment to delay rewards, and a purified spirit ought not to be further punished.

CHAPTER THREE

THE ANTECEDENTS OF THE JUDGMENT: INTERCESSIONS OF THE CHURCH

1. We must hold these truths about intercessions of the Church: that the intercessions of the Church benefit the dead. The intercessions which the Church makes for the dead are sacrifices, fastings, alms, and other prayers and voluntarily assumed sufferings for the quicker and easier expiation of their sins. They benefit the dead, not indiscriminately but only the "moderately good," those who are in purgatory. They do not benefit "the thoroughly evil," those who are in hell, or "the thoroughly good," [5] those who are in heaven. Rather their merits and prayers redound to the Church militant for whose members the saints seek many benefits. These intercessions give more or less aid either on account of the diversity of the merits of the dead or on account of the charity of the living which operates more in favor of some than of others. They are for the mitigation of suffering or the acceleration of the time of freedom according as the disposition of supernal providence shall see fit to expedite matters in their best interests.

2. The explanation of this is as follows: Because the first principle, since it is best and hence shows the greatest severity to the wicked, ought equally to show the greatest gentleness to the good, hence, since by reason of the severity of justice the just in whom there still is the guilt of sin ought after this life to be punished in purgatory, they ought also by reason of the gentleness of mercy to be raised again and to have aid and protection especially since they are enduring misery and can no longer aid themselves by their own works and merits. Hence the guidance of divine providence ought to direct that

[5] Peter Lombard, *Quattuor libri sententiarum*, IV, 45, 2; Augustine, *Enchiridion*, CIX, 29.

intercessions be conferred on the dead by those who can do so, maintaining nevertheless the rectitude of justice from which the gentleness of divine mercy ought not to depart and cannot depart or be in any way separated. Because the rectitude of justice demands the preservation of divine honor, of the order of the universe, and of the quality of human merit, the supreme providence of the supernal and first principle directs that those intercessions aid the dead as required by the gentleness of mercy and the order of justice in a manner consistent with the preservation of the dignity of divine honor, the order of the universe, and the quality of human merit.

3. In the first place, because justice ought to be served by such intercessions, for justice certainly maintains divine honor, and divine honor clearly requires works of satisfaction and penance to be performed for the dead on account of their faults, intercessions arise through these works and through them satisfaction is fully made and honor done to God. Because there are three such kinds of satisfaction, namely, fasting, prayer, and alms, and the sacrifice of the altar by which a fitting honor is most particularly rendered to God because of the pleasing quality of Him who is offered in that sacrifice, hence the intercessions of the Church consist in such works of satisfaction and especially in the celebration of Masses, as Gregory states in his fourth dialogue: "Some are most quickly freed from great sufferings because of the benefits of Masses." [6] Hence the pomp of the obsequies and the carefulness of the funeral and such things ought not to be reckoned as intercessions of the Church. For St. Augustine says in his book *De cura pro mortuis agenda* that "the performance of the funeral, the condition of the tomb, and the splendor of obsequies are more the consolation of the living than aids of the dead." [7]

4. Further, because justice which preserves order and gov-

[6] Gregory, *Dialogus*, IV, 55.
[7] Augustine, *De cura pro mortuis agenda*, II, 4.

ernment in the universe ought to be preserved itself, and this requires that in the communication of influence an order be preserved and that there be a symbol among those things from which and into which those influences flow, and because as a result what is inferior ought not to influence what is above or what is altogether remote, the intercessions of the Church cannot be of value to those who are in hell, because they are utterly separated from the mystical body of Christ and hence no spiritual influence reaches them or profits them, just as no influence of the head affects members severed from the body. Hence it also follows that the intercessions of the Church do not benefit the saints, because they are entirely superior as regards their status and, having achieved their terminus, they are unable to ascend higher but rather conversely they and their prayers benefit us for they gained their merits while alive. Hence divine order so disposed things that prayers are offered by the saints of God to aid us in our quest for divine benefits. The intercessions of the Church do not aid them, but rather their intercessions aid us. All that remains is that they benefit only the just who are undergoing purgatorial punishments. By reason of punishment and inability to help themselves, they are below those who are alive; by reason of justice they are bound to the other members of the Church so that the merits of holy Church can rightly be allotted to them because of symbol and order.

5. Finally, because justice ought to be achieved in them and justice considers the exigency of their merits, these intercessions which are made in common for the dead, though they may benefit all the good in a measure, more fully benefit those who have greater merits since they benefited and aided themselves while they were in the state of the wayfarer. Those merits which are directed to particular persons benefit more those for whom they are definitely intended since the intention of the one interceding is upright and God proceeds accordingly and the ecclesiastical institution is certainly not empty. Yet

in some way they are passed on to others also. But they cannot aid others in the same way as they do the designated person since, though they are spiritual merits, yet divine justice demands greater satisfaction for a greater fault, and many satisfactions for many faults. Hence the example of light which spreads equally over all sitting at one table is not fitting because these intercessions have to be likened to rewards of redemption rather than to diffusive influence. Hence one has to define clearly to what extent intercessions should definitely aid anyone, and to look to the gravity, number, and measure of the crimes, their punishments, and the intercessions therefor.

CHAPTER FOUR

THE CONCOMITANTS OF THE JUDGMENT: THE BURNING OF THE FIRES

1. We ought to add something about the concomitants of the judgment; and they are two, namely, the burning of the fires mundane and the resurrection of the body.

2. We must hold these truths about the burning of the fires: that fire precedes the face of the judge and will consume the face of the earth so that the fashion of this world will perish in the burning of the mundane fires just as it was destroyed by the inundation of the flood. The fashion of this world is not said to pass away because of the complete destruction of this world of sense, but because, by the action of that fire in burning, all things elemental, things vegetative and animal, will be consumed and the elements purified and renewed, especially air and earth. The just will be purified and the wicked will be scorched. With these things accomplished, the motion of the heavens will cease so that thus, in a com-

plete enumeration of the elect, there will be a resurrection and rewarding in some way of their earthly bodies.

3. The explanation of this is as follows: Since the universal principle of things is most wise and though He pursues the path of wisdom in all He does, yet He ought especially to pursue that path in matters related to the consummation of things so that He does not displace the first by the middle or the middle by the last, but that the ordaining wisdom, goodness, and highness of the first principle may appear in all things most orderly arranged. Because God in accord with His most ordinate wisdom made the whole world of life, the greater world, because of a lesser world, namely, man, who is allotted a place between God and things inferior, hence in order that all might be mutually congruous and that the inhabitation of the world might be in harmony with the inhabitant, since man was well created, the world ought to have been created in a good and quiet way. But with the fall of man, that world ought to have deteriorated, and with the presence of turmoil in man that world ought to have been stirred up, and with the purification of man it ought to have been purified, and with the renovation of man it ought to have been renovated, and with the consummation of man it ought to have been put to rest.

4. First, because that world ought to be stirred up when turmoil settles on man, just as it stood while he stood and in a way fell when he fell, and because in the future judgment because of the severity which the judge will show, there will necessarily be terror in the hearts of all and especially in the hearts of sinners who have rejected the Lord of all, the poles of the whole earth must be moved most terribly so that every creature will accept the divine zeal and be conformed to his Author and to the inhabitant. And because nothing is more intense, more swift, and more horrible in its motion in disturbing other elements than fire springing up on every quar-

ter, fire will necessarily precede the face of the Judge not on one side alone but in every part of the world so that there may be a concourse of elemental and terrestrial fire, of the fire of purgatory and of hell, so that the wicked may be scorched by the fire of hell, the just purified by the fire of purgatory, those things born of the earth consumed by the terrestrial fire, and the elements revamped by the elemental fire and arranged for the appearance of the innovation, and at the same time all other things will be thrown into turmoil so that not alone man and demons but even angels will be terrified at the sight.

5. Again, because the world ought to be purified with the purification of man, and man at the end of time needs to be purged of the dross of avarice and malice, just as in the beginning of time he needed to be purged of the dross of luxury, and man needs to be purged swiftly, to the very core and perfectly, hence, just as the world was earlier laid waste and in some way purified by the element of water, which is cold, opposed to ardor and the dross of luxury, so the world at the end of time will be purified by fire because of the cooling of our charity and the cold of malice and avarice which shall rule in the end as if in the old age of the world. Because these ills cling most closely, the purification must occur by an innermost, violent, and swift action, and these qualities do not happen to be found in any other element than fire. Hence, just as there was an inundation by the flood, so the appearance of the world of sense will be consumed by fire.

6. Further, because the world ought to be renovated when man is renovated and nothing can be changed to a new form unless it loses its old form and in some way is arranged in a new, superimposed plan, hence, since fire certainly has the power of expelling an extraneous form and is a force endowed with subtility and related to celestial nature, the purification and renovation ought simultaneously to be accom-

plished by it so that, since it possesses a dual efficacy, it precedes the advent of the Judge in some respect and must follow Him in another. Since the renovation is intended to achieve a newness which no longer lapses into antiquity and this is to achieve an incorruptible newness which no creature can do, it follows that, though some of that purification and renovation by fire may be achieved by a natural power such as the spreading of the flames, their purifying effect, their rarification, and their intensity, yet there must be operating with that natural power a supernatural power whose order causes the beginning of the conflagration and by whose power the whole is achieved.

7. Finally, because the world ought to be consumed when man faces consummation, and man is to be consumed when the number of the elect in glory shall be complete and all tend to this state as their ultimate and complete end, it follows that upon the completion of that process there must be an end to the motion of celestial nature and quiet in it, and likewise elemental transmutations must cease and consequently generation both animal and vegetative must cease. Since all these matters are subordinated to the most noble form, which is the rational soul, hence, by virtue of its place among spirits, its status and complement must be established in other precedents. Hence the celestial bodies in a quiet and a fullness of light are said to be rewarded. The elements which no longer have the power of multiplying by a mutual transmutation are said to perish not alone as regards their substance but as regards their mutual activity and passivity, and most especially as regards their active qualities. Things vegetative and things sensitive, since they do not possess the power of perpetual life and eternal duration, for such is the degree of their nobility, must be consumed in their own natures and yet in such a way that they are saved in their principles and somehow in likeness, namely, in man who has a likeness to

every kind of creature. Hence in man's renovation and glorification we can speak of the renovation of all and in some fashion of the reward of all.

CHAPTER FIVE

THE CONCOMITANTS OF THE JUDGMENT: THE RESURRECTION OF OUR BODIES

1. We must hold these truths about the resurrection of our
bodies: that the bodies of all men will arise in a general resurrection, no interval existing between them as regards time
order but a great distance between them as regards dignity.
The evil will rise with their deformities and punishments,
miserable, and with the defects they had in life. In the good,
however, "nature will be preserved and faults done away
with" [8] and they will all rise with an unimpaired body in the
prime of life and with suitable coordination of their members
so that all the saints will meet in perfect manhood in the age
of the fullness of Christ. Suitably, bodies will rise the same
in the case of the good and in the case of the evil as they existed earlier, and from the same parts, and the truth of all nature will be preserved not alone as regards the principal members and the radical humor but even down to the last hair
and other members which contribute to the comeliness of
the body so that, "though the dust of the human body may be
spread to distant breezes and shores, it will return to that soul
which it first served so that it may live, grow, and breathe." [9]

2. The explanation of this is as follows: The first principle,
by the very fact that it is first and highest, is the most universal
and sufficient and hence the principle of natures, of grace,
and of rewards, a principle most potent, most clement, and

---

[8] Augustine, *De civitate Dei*, XXII, 17.
[9] *Ibid.*, *Enchiridion*, LXXXVIII, 23.

most just, and though in accord with a certain appropriation the principle is most potent in establishing natures and most clement in the coordination of graces and most just in its retribution, yet single things exist in single persons because the highest power, clemency, and justice cannot be separated one from another. Hence in the work of retribution that must be so in accord with the exigency of the rectitude of justice, the reformation by grace, and the fulfillment of nature. Because justice necessarily requires that, as man, who deserves merit or demerit not in soul alone but in both soul and body, should be punished or rewarded in both, and because the reformation of grace requires that man's whole body shall be likened to Christ, the head, whose dead body had to arise since it was inseparably united to His divinity, and because the fulfillment of nature requires that man be reorganized in body and soul as matter and form which possess a mutual appetite and inclination, it follows that the resurrection will occur in the future by the exigency of the plan of nature, the infusion of grace, and the retribution of justice, for the whole universe must be governed according to these. Hence for these three reasons, all things demand that man arise so that every excuse may be leveled for those who were deaf to the truth of faith, and the whole world may fight against such.

3. First, because the resurrection ought to follow the dictates of the order of divine justice, and divine justice renders to each what is his at the place and time, and every soul once with a body and at the end of time united again thereto possesses either sin or grace, all must necessarily arise. Because there ought to be a distinction between the state of retribution and that of life, the resurrection belongs to the state of retribution that the order of the universe may not be confused and that faith may claim its reward, for faith believes what it does not see, and likewise the resurrection belongs to the state of retribution in order that the equity of divine justice may be more certainly and clearly demonstrated, and in or-

der that there may simultaneously be a consummation and final retribution for angels and men. Divine justice requires that there should arise at the same time all those who are under the common law. I refer to the common law because of Christ and His most blessed mother, the glorious Virgin Mary. Because punishment and misery are the lot of the wicked, and glory the lot of the good, it follows that, though they must rise at the same time, they will be completely dissimilar in their condition. Because the wicked do not arise for life eternal but for punishment, they must arise with their infirmities, deformities, and defects.

4. Again, because the resurrection ought to follow the exigency of the consummation of grace, and perfect grace makes us conform to Christ, our head, and there is no defect in His members but perfect maturity, suitable stature, and a well-formed image, it is fitting that the good should rise in the very best condition. This means that they should lack defects and that their nature should be preserved. It is also fitting that if any member is lacking it should be supplied, if there is a superfluity it should be dispensed with, if there is any disorder among the members it should be corrected, if something is too small it should be led by divine power to achieve the stature Christ had in the resurrection "though not in that degree," [10] if anyone is decrepit he should be restored to the same stature, if someone is a giant or a dwarf he should be reduced or raised to suitable stature so that all may be whole and all perfect when they meet in the perfect man, in the fullness of the age of Christ.

5. Finally, because the resurrection ought to follow the exigency of the perfection of nature, and the nature of a rational spirit requires that it vivify its own body because "a proper act must be accomplished in the proper matter,[11] it follows necessarily that for that purpose the same bodies will

[10] *Ibid., De civitate Dei*, XXII, 14.
[11] Aristotle, *De anima*, II, 2.

rise, otherwise there would not be a true resurrection. The nature of the rational and immortal soul requires that, as it has a perpetual existence, so it should have a body to which it may forever give life. Thus the body which is united to the soul from that very union derives an eternal incorruptibility and yet in such a way that that in which the substance of the whole body consists, namely, its principal members and the radical humor and flesh in species, possess the necessary design, but the other members, namely, flesh according to matter and those parts of the body which contribute to its nice existence, have a congruous design. Hence the primary parts of the body are intended for a resurrection in the order of necessity, but all the other parts follow the order of congruity. Because God imposed this order on nature, for nature cannot achieve it, being unable to raise the dead, and because divine providence ought not to have done anything in vain, the same body must be restored by His power suitably and immortally and arranged with all its parts and the complete truth of nature thereby preserved. Since nature does not have these things in its power but only in its appetite, for it cannot repair the same body once destroyed, and since nature cannot restore the whole substance of a thing nor can it bring the body to immortality since all that is generated by nature is corruptible, and since nature cannot gather what has been scattered, the resurrection must be attributed not to seminal or natural causes but to primordial causes that it may follow the wonderful and supernatural course and the command of the divine will.

CHAPTER SIX

THE CONSEQUENTS OF THE JUDGMENT: THE INFERNAL PUNISHMENT

1. We must hold this about the consequents of judgment: that they are two: infernal punishment and heavenly glory.

2. We must hold these truths about infernal punishment: that infernal punishment takes place down below in a place corporeal where all the wicked are eternally tortured, evil men as well as spirits. They are tortured by the same corporeal fire which will burn and torture spirits and bodies alike. But the fire will not consume bodies but rather will eternally torture them—some more, some less according to the exigency of their merits. To torture of this kind of fire will be joined torture of all the senses and the punishment of a worm and the lack of the sight of God with the result that in these punishments there will be a variety, and with variety a severity, and with severity an eternity, so that from the punishment of the wicked "the smoke of their torments shall ascend up forever and ever." [12]

3. The explanation of this is as follows: Because the first principle, which by the very fact that it is first is highest, possesses in the highest degree whatever it possesses, it must be most upright. Since in retribution it acts in accord with uprightness just as it cannot act contrary to itself and cannot deny itself and cannot oppose its own justice, it ought necessarily, because of the exigency of rectitude, to punish sin according to the amount of fault. It ought to punish particularly those who show contempt for the law of mercy and by impenitence dash themselves against the severity of His justice. Because in calculating the severity of His justice He considers not only the origin of the fault but its aggravating circum-

[12] Apoc. 14:11.

…ost fitting that the just judge exact the punish-
…m the wicked down to the last farthing so that
…ot remain "the impropriety of sin without the
…stice." [13] Thus, as His power is manifest in
…isdom in government, and His clemency in
…His justice is manifest in punishment. Because
…ught to punish the wicked sinner according
…of his sin, and a mortal sin which is followed
…nce carries with it perpetual, licentious, and
…ler, such a soul must be punished with eter-
…nultiform punishments.

…place, the punishment for perpetual disor-
…ernal because a sin one commits and never
…rever in the soul and separates it from life
…om God, and proceeds from a will that
… enjoy itself in sin. Though such an en-
…ry, yet because its disorder has the quality
…unishment due for the disorder ought to
…at, as man in his eternal sin does not end
…drawing from sin, so God in Himself per-
… punishing. And as man sinned against
…ffers infinite punishment. And because
…nishment infinite in intensity, he must
…nd as man's will after death inheres for-
…undertaking penance, so God tortures
…y change of sentence because of the per-
…he damned.

…he punishment of licentious disorder
…since enjoyment is punished by an op-
… the rational spirit by sinning turns
…ving the present and licentious, and
…ne command and order, hence that
…perfectly punished, for it is enjoy-
…tempt, it is necessary that, for the

…, III, 15, 44.

punishment of that contempt and enjoyment, the si
whether man or spirit be plunged into the nether regio
removed from the state of glory, and this is to the most
found depths. It is necessary that the one to be torment
his lower nature be there exposed to torment and h
should not undergo punishment by a spiritual substanc
only by a corporeal and lower substance, i.e., by the dr
mundane bodies, for he is settled in his lees and torm
with fire and brimstone.[14] And because the spirit, whi
nature holds preference over the body and has to invi
the body and motivates it, perverted the dignity of nat
sin and subjected man in a certain way to the vilene
nothingness of sin, it follows that in accord with the
of justice things ought to be so ordained that the sinn
is spirit should be bound to a corporeal fire as well a
not that it imbues that sinner with life but that th
son may receive the punishment divinely ordered. Si
soul is inseparably bound to the body and terrifies t
with a divinely implanted fear and endows it with s
through the power of a natural sense, it must be seve
mented. And because that fire only affects one who
in sin, fault, and its aftermath owing to the improbity
centiousness that goes before, and not all are guil
same degree, some are burnt more and others less th
fire is the same, just as the same fire burns dross in
and wood in another. Because the degree of sin and
erning the moderation of fire is uniform and never
decreases, or changes in the same person, the fire
command acts in such a way that it forever burns
not consume, forever tortures and is without end
does not try to make its own form grow but tries t
peace in the body or of the spirit itself. Hence th
not be a new deprivation of peace but a continua
deprivation of peace for in that very punishme

14 Apoc. 14:10.

should not take precedence over eternity or eternity take precedence over severity.

6. Finally, because the punishment for manifold disorder ought to be manifold, and in all actual mortal sin there is a disordered aversion from the supreme light and goodness and an inordinate turning to the commutable good and a disorder of the will which is in conflict with the dictates of right reason, hence all those guilty of actual sin who will be damned will be punished with a threefold punishment: because of their aversion from God they suffer the loss of the sight of God; because of the turning to commutable good they receive the punishment of a material fire; because of the conflict of will and reason they receive the punishment of a worm, so that thus they are afflicted by a multiplicity of punishments and tortured in many ways, severely and eternally, and the smoke of their torments will ascend forever and ever. Amen.

CHAPTER SEVEN

THE GLORY OF PARADISE

1. We must hold these truths about the heavenly glory: that in it there is a reward substantial, consubstantial, and accidental. The substantial reward consists in the vision, enjoyment, and possession of the one highest good, namely, God, whom the blessed will see face to face, that is, plainly and without a veil, whom they will enjoy eagerly and agreeably, whom they will possess eternally, as the statement of Bernard establishes: "God in the future is a fullness of light in the reason, a fullness of peace in the will, and a continuation of eternity in the memory." [15] The consubstantial reward consists in the glory of the body, which is said to be a second stole. After resuming that glory of the body, the blessed soul seeks more

[15] Bernard, *Sermo* XI.

perfectly the highest heaven. This stole consists in a fourfold
endowment of the body, namely, in an endowment of per-
spicacity, subtlety, agility, and impassibility, which qualities
will be greater or less according as previously charity had been
greater or less. The accidental reward consists of a certain special and extra embellishment which is called golden and, according to the opinion of the learned, is due to three achieve-
ments, namely, martyrdom, prophecy, and continency. In all
these a gradation and distinction due to merits will be preserved.

2. The explanation of this is as follows: The first principle,
by the very fact that it is first, possesses the greatest unity,
truth, and goodness, and this means it has the greatest power,
wisdom, clemency, and justice. Because these invisible qualities of God ought to be made manifest by works, God so produced the sensible world at the outset, so governs, so redeems,
so rewards and ends it that the greatest power is evident in its
production, wisdom in its government, clemency in its redemption, and justice is achieved in retribution. That power
might be manifested He produced all from nothing for His
praise, glory, and honor, making something bordering on
nothing, namely, corporeal matter, and something bordering
on Himself, namely, spiritual substance, and joined these
simultaneously in one man in a unity of nature and person,
namely, by joining the rational soul and corporeal matter.
That He might show His wisdom, He governs all most provi-
dently and orderly. He governs the supreme part of man by
man himself, namely, by his mind, which He illumines. He
governs the lower part, namely, the body, by free choice of
his will so that as long as the body and things corporeal obey
the spirit, the spirit may subject them to God. That He might
show His clemency, God redeemed man after his fall by assuming the nature of man, by undertaking sufferings, and
finally by bearing punishment so that thus the greatest mercy
might show to miserable man a mercy designed to alleviate

the misery of man not alone in the dignity of man's nature as created but also in the defects of that nature as confined to misery. Finally that He might show His justice He requites each according to the exigency of his merits: punishment to the wicked and eternal glory to the just. Equitable recompense, a gratuitous redemption, an orderly government, and a production evidencing power demanded such. The consummation of all these is achieved in the end.

3. First, because the reward of all the just ought to come about as required by a just recompense and a production showing power and because God's production made the rational spirit like God, capable of God, capable in accord with the power of the inborn image of the most Blessed Trinity itself, for the whole spirit of the just man is directed to the Trinity according to the integrity of his image, it follows that nothing less than God can reward or satisfy the rational spirit, nor can its capacity be exhausted by less. Hence in man's reward that godliness of glory is given him by which he is conformed to God, sees God clearly with his reason, loves God fully with his will, and retains Him forever in his memory. Thus the whole soul lives, the whole soul is richly endowed in its three powers, the whole soul is joined to God, is united to Him and rests in Him, finding in Him as in all good, peace, light, and eternal sufficiency. Hence, situated "in the state of all good in a perfect gathering" [16] and achieving eternal life, man is said to be happy and glorious.

4. And, because that retribution ought to occur not only as the exigency of just retribution and powerful production require but also as well-planned government requires, and because God in producing the body bound it to the soul and joined to it a natural and mutual appetite and subjected it to government and placed it in a state of merit so that the spirit might direct and guide the government of the body and gain merit by its exercise, it follows that the natural ap-

[16] Boethius, *De consolatione philosophiae*, III, 2.

petite did not allow the soul to be replete in happiness unless
the soul guided the body there too, for the spirit has a tendency naturally implanted to rejoin the body, nor did orderly
government permit the body to rejoin the happy spirit unless
the body was made subject to and congruous with the soul
in everything in so far as the body can be conformed to the
soul. Because the spirit is clarified by the sight of the eternal
light, exceeding keenness of light ought to result in the body.
Because the spiritual effect in summa lies in the enjoyment
of His most high spirit, there ought to be a corresponding
acuteness and spirituality in the body. Because by possessing
eternity man is made completely passionless, there ought to
be in the body a complete external and internal lack of passion. Because the spirit is made most agile in its quest of God
by all these qualities, the greatest agility ought to be found
in the glorified body. Because by these four properties the
body is made to conform to the spirit and is made subject to
it, the body is said to be particularly endowed by these four,
and as a result of these the body is adapted to following the
spirit and to being situate in the heavenly arena which is the
province of the blessed. In these properties the body resembles
the heavenly bodies for by these qualities a heavenly body is
removed in degree from the four elements. Thus with its fourfold dowry the body reappears with perfection and conformity
to the heavenly way and to the Holy Ghost, through whom a
fullness of sweetness and an overflowing of happiness run
down from the very head of God to the bottom of His garment,
namely, the body, and as much as possible is thereby gained.

5. Finally, because the reward ought to occur as required
by the exigency of a just retribution, a powerful production,
a well-designed government, and even a glorious redemption,
and because the gifts of graces are divided among the diverse
members of Christ as regards internal gifts and as regards their
external use, with respect not only to one's infused virtue
but also to one's status, not only with regard to the perfection

of charity in the mind but also with regard to the elegance of perfection and the beauty in bodily movement, it follows that there ought to be given to some members not only the stole of the soul with its three gifts and the stole of the body with its four, but also a certain superiority in elegance and joy because of the excellence of their perfection and the elegance they acquired in their powerful work. Because their work has three features, being excellently perfect, beautiful, and endowed with a special gracefulness corresponding to the triple power of the soul so that there flows from their rational power the publication of truth leading others to salvation, from their concupiscible power a perfect denial of things concupiscent by perpetual maintenance of continence, and from their irascible power a suffering of death for the honor of Christ, it follows that the excellence of an accidental reward which is called golden ought to belong to three kinds of the just, namely, to those giving public testimony, to virgins, and to martyrs. And this reward adds to the elegance not only of the soul but of the body because it enhances not only the will but its extrinsic work, reflecting on itself merit and the reward of charity which consists in a sevenfold endowment: a triple endowment of the soul and a fourfold endowment of the body, and in these are included the consummation, integrity, and fullness of all good referring to the end of glory.

6. In these words and at such length not I, but blessed Anselm, has described these matters. In the end of his *Proslogium* [17] he says:

Now, my soul, arouse and lift up all your understanding and conceive, if you can, what character that good has and how great it is. If individual goods are delectable, strive to imagine how delectable is that good which contains the enjoyment of all goods, not such as we have experienced in created objects, but as different as the Creator from the creature. If the created life is good, how good is the creative life? If the salvation granted is delightful, how

[17] Anselm, *Proslogium,* chaps. 24 f.

delightful is the salvation which has given all salvation? If wisdom in the knowledge of the created world is sweet, how sweet is the wisdom which has created all things from nothing? Lastly, if there are many great delights in pleasurable things, how fine and how great is the delight in Him who has made these delightful things?

7. Who shall enjoy this good? What shall belong to him and what shall not belong to him? Whatever he shall want shall be his and whatever he shall not want shall not be his. The goods of body and soul will be such as eye hath not seen and ear heard, neither has the heart of man conceived.[18]

Why do you wander abroad, little man, in search of the goods of soul and body? Love the one good in which are all goods, and it is enough. Seek the simple good which is all good, and it is enough. What do you love, my flesh? What do you seek, my soul? There is whatever you love, whatever you seek.

If beauty delights them, there "shall the just shine as the sun." [19] If swiftness or endurance or freedom of body, which nothing can withstand, delight them, they shall be as angels of God [20]—because though "it is sown a natural body, it shall rise a spiritual body" [21]— in power certainly, though not in nature. If it is a long and sound life that pleases them, there is a healthy eternity and an eternal health because the righteous shall live forever [22] and "the salvation of the just is from the Lord." [23] If it is satisfaction of hunger, they shall be satisfied when the glory of the Lord has appeared.[24] If it is quenching of thirst, they shall be abundantly satisfied with the plenty of God's house.[25] If it is melody, there the choir of angels sings forever before God. If it is anything not impure, but pure pleasure, Thou shalt make them drink of the river of Thy pleasure, O God.[26]

If it is wisdom that delights them, the very wisdom of God will reveal itself to them. If friendship, they shall love God more than themselves, and one another as themselves. God shall love

18 I Cor. 2:9.
19 Matt. 13:43.
20 Ibid., 22:30.
21 I Cor. 15:44.
22 Wisd. 5:16.
23 Ps. 36:39.
24 Ibid., 16:15.
25 Ibid., 35:9.
26 Ibid.

them more than they themselves, for they love Him and themselves and one another through Him, and He loves Himself and
them through Himself. If they seek agreement, they shall all have
a single will because they will have no will but God's will.

If they seek power, they shall have all power to fulfill their
will, as God has to fulfill His. As God has power to do what He
wills, through Himself, so they will have power, through Him, to
do what they will. Since they will not will anything except what
He wills, He shall will whatever they will, and what He shall will
cannot fail to be. If honor and riches are their delight, God shall
make His good and faithful servants rulers over many things.[27]
They shall be called the children of God [28] and gods. Where His
Son shall be, there also shall be "the heirs indeed of God and
joint heirs with Christ." [29]

If true security delights them, undoubtedly they will be as sure
that these goods, or rather that good, will never fail them, as they
will be sure that they will not lose it of their own accord. That
God, who loves them, will not take it away against the will of
those who love Him. Nothing more powerful than God will
separate Him from them against His will and theirs.

8. But what a joy and how great it is, where is there a good
of such a kind or so great? Heart of man, needy heart, heart ac-
quainted with sorrows, overwhelmed with sorrows, how greatly
would you rejoice if you abounded in all these things? Ask your
inner self whether it could contain its joy over so great a blessedness for itself.

Yet, if anyone else whom you love as much as yourself possessed
the same blessedness, your joy would be doubled because you
would rejoice as much for him as for yourself. If two or many more
have the same joy, you would rejoice as much for each one as for
yourself, if you love each as yourself. Thus in that perfect love of
innumerable blessed angels and sainted men where none will
love another less than himself, everyone will rejoice for each of the
others as for himself.

If the heart of man will scarcely contain his joy over his own
great good, how will it contain so many great joys? Because everyone rejoices as much in another's good as he loves the other, it
follows that, as in perfect happiness each one undoubtedly will

[27] Matt. 25:21.
[28] *Ibid.*, 5:9.
[29] Rom. 8:17.

love God beyond comparison and more than himself and all the others with himself, so he will rejoice beyond measure in the happiness of God, more than in his own and that of all the others with him.

If they will so love God with all their heart and all their mind and all their soul, still all their heart and all their mind and all their soul will not suffice for the worthiness of this love. Surely they will so rejoice with all their heart and all their mind and all their soul that all their heart and all their mind and all their soul will not suffice for the fullness of their joy.

9. Not yet, then, have I told or conceived, O Lord, how greatly Your blessed shall rejoice. They will rejoice according as they will love, and they will love according as they will know. How far will they know You, Lord, and how much will they love You? Truly eye has not seen nor ear heard, nor has it entered into the heart of man in this life how much they will know You and love You in that life.

I pray, O God, to know You, to love You, that I may rejoice in You. If I cannot attain full joy in this life, may I at least advance from day to day until that joy becomes full. May the knowledge of You advance in me here, and there be made full. May love of You increase here, and there be full that here my joy may be great in hope and there full in fact. Lord, through Your Son You command, You counsel us to ask, and You promise that we shall receive that our joy may be full. I ask, true Lord, that I may be granted that my joy be full. I ask, O Lord, as You counsel through the wonderful Counsellor, that I receive what You promise by virtue of Your truth, that my joy may be full. Meanwhile, let my mind meditate upon it, let my tongue speak of it, let my heart love it, let my mouth talk of it, let my soul hunger for it, let my flesh thirst for it, let my whole being desire it until I enter into the joy of my Lord who is the Three and the One God, "who is blessed forever. Amen." [30]

[30] Rom. 1:25.

GENERAL INDEX

INDEX OF WORKS CITED